THE TRAGEDY OF

Coriolanus

A BLAISDELL BOOK

IN THE HUMANITIES

EDITED BY
George Lyman Kittredge

Revised by Irving Ribner

William Shakespeare

THE TRAGEDY OF

Coriolanus

BLAISDELL PUBLISHING COMPANY

A Division of Ginn and Company

WALTHAM, MASSACHUSETTS · TORONTO · LONDON

PREFACE

The New Kittredge Shakespeares

The publication of George Lyman Kittredge's *Complete Works of Shakespeare* in 1936 was a landmark in Shakespeare scholarship. The teacher who for almost half a century had dominated and shaped the direction of Shakespearean study in America produced what was recognized widely as the finest edition of Shakespeare up to his time. In the preface to this edition Kittredge indicated his editorial principles; these allowed a paramount authority to the Folio of 1623 and countenanced few departures from it while, at the same time, refusing to "canonize the heedless type-setters of the Elizabethan printing house." Kittredge's work was marked by a judicious conservatism and a common sense rarely found in equal measure in earlier editors of Shakespeare. In the thirty-odd years which have gone by since the appearance of this monumental volume, however, considerable advances have been made in the establishment of Shakespeare's text, and our body of knowledge about the dates, sources, and general historical background of Shakespeare's plays has vastly increased. The present revision is designed to apply this new knowledge to Kittredge's work so that it may have as much value to the student and general reader of today as it had to those of thirty years ago.

Before his death Kittredge had issued, in addition to *The Complete Works,* separate editions of sixteen of the plays, each copiously annotated. Some of the notes were unusually elaborate, but they interpreted Shakespeare's language with a fullness and precision attained by few other commentators, for Kittredge had few equals in his intimate knowledge of Elizabethan English. In freshly annotating the plays I have, accordingly, tried to use

Kittredge's own notes as fully as space would permit. Where I have repeated his distinctive language or recorded his characteristic critical opinions, I have followed the note with the symbol [K]; where Kittredge's definition of a term can be found in essentially the same words in other editions, I have not used the identifying symbol. Every annotator draws upon the full body of the notes of earlier editors, and to give credit for every note is impossible. Notes have been placed at page bottoms.

The brief introductions which Kittredge wrote for the plays have been replaced by new ones, for what seemed like indisputable fact some thirty years ago often appears today to be much more uncertain, and many new issues of which Kittredge was not aware have been raised in recent criticism. The new introductions seek to present what are now generally agreed to be basic facts about the plays and to give some indications of the directions which modern criticism has taken, although specific analyses of individual plays are avoided.

Such great authority attaches to Kittredge's text that it has not frequently — and never lightly — been departed from. Where changes have been made, they have usually involved the restoration of copy-text readings now generally accepted in place of the emendations of eighteenth- and nineteenth-century editors of which Kittredge, in spite of his extraordinary conservatism in this regard, sometimes too easily approved. Only rarely has an emendation been adopted in the present revision which was not also adopted by Kittredge. All departures from the copy-texts are indicated in the notes, emendations followed by the names of the editors by whom they were first proposed. Wherever Kittredge's text has been departed from for any reason, his reading is given in the notes. Modern spelling has in a few instances been substituted for Elizabethan forms which are mere spelling variations but which Kittredge nevertheless retained. His punctuation has not been altered except in a few very rare instances.

The system of recording elisions and contractions which Kittredge explained in his introduction to *The Complete Works* has been retained, as has his method of preserving to the fullest the copy-text stage directions, with all additions to them enclosed within square brackets. Although modern editors recog-

nize the vagueness of the place settings of Elizabethan plays and
are reluctant to include the place designations so favoured by
eighteenth- and nineteenth-century editors, much historical inter-
est nevertheless attaches to these, and Kittredge's place designations accordingly have been retained between square brackets.
Kittredge's attempt to retain the line numbering of the Globe
text, which resulted in considerable irregularity in prose passages,
has been abandoned, and the lines of each play have been freshly
numbered. Kittredge's act and scene divisions have been retained,
as has his practice of surrounding by square brackets those divisions which are not in the copy-texts.

The plan of *The New Kittredge Shakespeares* is a comprehensive one. They will include a new edition of *The Complete
Works* and individual editions of each of the plays, the sonnets,
and the poems. A comprehensive introduction to Shakespeare's
life, times, and theatrical milieu will be published both as a
separate volume and as an introduction to *The Complete Works*.

IRVING RIBNER

INTRODUCTION

The Tragedy of Coriolanus

◇◇◇◇◇
◇◇◇◇◇   We do not know exactly when *Coriolanus* was written,
◇◇◇◇◇   and we know virtually nothing of its early stage history.
There is no record of a production before that of an adaptation
by Nahum Tate, called *The Ingratitude of a Commonwealth, or
The Fall of Coriolanus,* which was published in 1682. Stylistic
considerations make it clear, however, that it must have been
among Shakespeare's later tragedies, probably following close
upon *Antony and Cleopatra* and springing from the same return
to Roman history which had resulted in that play. *Coriolanus*
must have been written later than 1605 because Menenius' fable
of the belly and the members (I.i.82–132), although widely current in many forms, is directly influenced by a version in
William Camden's *Remaines concerning Britaine,* published in
1605. A probable allusion to the play in Ben Jonson's *The Silent
Woman,* written in 1610, would suggest that *Coriolanus* had
been on the stage for some time by that year. A more certain
echo of the play, however, appears in Robert Armin's *The
Italian Taylor and his Boy,* printed in 1609. Here lines I.i.198–9
seem to be recollected in Armin's words: "A strange time of
taxation, wherein euery Pen and inck-horne Boy will throw vp
his Cap at the hornes of the Moone in censure, although his wit
hang there, not returning vnless monthly in the wane." Since
Armin was a member of Shakespeare's company and is known to
have acted in some of Shakespeare's plays (*Twelfth Night* and
As You Like It, for instance), it is virtually certain that he wrote
with *Coriolanus* in mind.

Most scholars would thus date the play in late 1607 or 1608.
A series of insurrections in the Midlands, including Shakespeare's

own Warwickshire, which took place in May and June of 1607 and were directed largely against the enclosure of grazing commons, would have given the play considerable topicality at that time, and some have suggested, in fact, that *Coriolanus* may have been inspired by Shakespeare's own experience with these uprisings of the poor. E. C. Pettet has argued in *Shakespeare Survey 3* (Cambridge: University Press, 1950), pp. 34–42, that Shakespeare altered his sources so as to make the uprising of the Plebeians in his play resemble more closely that which had taken place in his own native county. Further evidence of date is afforded by the reference at I.i.159 to "the coal of fire upon the ice," which may have been suggested by a severe frost in the winter of 1607–8, when pans of coals actually were placed upon the Thames in an attempt to thaw the frozen river.

The play was printed for the first time in the folio of 1623 (F[1]), as the first of the tragedies, either from Shakespeare's own manuscript or from a transcript of it. It is a text noteworthy for the fullness of its stage directions, but it is marred by a great number of printers' errors — most of them, fortunately, fairly easy to correct — and by extremely faulty lineation. It is divided into acts, but not into scenes, the divisions of the present text being those of the Globe editors. Otherwise F[1] is followed closely, all departures from it being indicated in the notes.

SOURCES

For the story of Coriolanus Shakespeare went to Sir Thomas North's translation of Plutarch's *Parallel Lives,* which had already served as his chief source for *Julius Cæsar* and *Antony and Cleopatra*. In the main he followed his source closely, although he made certain changes so as to heighten the dramatic intensity of his play and so as to shape the character of his hero in a way only partly suggested by Plutarch. Shakespeare compresses several uprisings and the events of a long period of time into a highly unified account which seems of relatively brief duration. In general, he minimizes the very real grievances of the common people, omitting their earlier departure from Rome and the commitments made to them before their return. Rather than have the banishment of Coriolanus result from one of the several uprisings over grain, as in Plutarch, he has it spring from his pursuit of the consulship, which in Plutarch does not occur until Coriolanus has already earned the enmity of the people by several other acts. The reluctance of Coriolanus to seek the office, the role of Volumnia in persuading him, and the arrogant rudeness of Coriolanus as an office-seeker are all Shakespeare's invention.

The characters of Menenius, Aufidius, and Volumnia are developed beyond anything in the source. In Plutarch Menenius appears only once; he tells the story of the belly and the members in an attempt to pacify the common people who have left the city in resentment over the Patricians, and he is instrumental in bringing about their return. Of the special relation between the hero and his mother which is so basic to Shakespeare's play, there is little suggestion in Plutarch, where the mother has almost no role before she leads the embassy of the women — actually the fourth such embassy to plead with Coriolanus — which is suggested by Valeria. The character of young Marcius is developed from the mere mention of the hero's children in the source.

The historical Coriolanus was a semilegendary figure belonging to the earliest period of Roman history. His story was told by Livy in the second book of his *Roman History,* as part of an account of the general discord following the expulsion of the Tarquins from Rome at the end of the fifth century, B.C., when dissention between Patricians and Plebeians was very strong, and when harsh treatment of debtors by usurers, among other economic abuses, was a constant source of civil turmoil. At the same time Rome was harassed by constant struggle against external enemies, including the tribe of Volsces, against whose city Coriolanus achieved his most notable victory. That Shakespeare had read the story of Coriolanus in Philemon Holland's translation of Livy, published in 1600, we can be fairly certain. In this account the hero has two young sons who appear with his mother, named Veturia, and his wife, named Volumnia, to plead with him for the sparing of Rome.

Many later versions of the story were based upon Livy, in-

cluding that in the *Roman Antiquities* of Dionysius of Helicar-
nassus, from whom Plutarch drew his account. It is unlikely that
this was known to Shakespeare, since no English translation ap-
peared during his lifetime. Dionysius introduced the character
of Valeria as the instigator of the embassy of women. A version
appears also in the *Roman Histories* of Lucius Florus, where an
account of Coriolanus serves to illustrate the petty feuding with
neighboring cities which marked the infancy of Rome. At least
one play on the subject had been written before Shakespeare
approached it. Alexandre Hardy had written a Senecan tragedy
in French called *Coriolan* around 1600. It was not published
until 1625, and Shakespeare is not likely to have known it, but
it is significant in that it treats the subject in simple terms as a
tragedy of aristocratic pride and thus offers some indication of
the general terms in which Coriolanus was viewed at the time
Shakespeare was writing. Like Shakespeare's play, Hardy's is
based closely upon Plutarch, and this may account for many of
the similarities between the two works.

THE BELLY AND THE MEMBERS

Menenius' fable of the belly and the members is an ancient political parable of Oriental origin. It is told both by Livy and by
Plutarch. Shakespeare read it in these places and in William
Camden's *Remaines*. There is a version in Sir Philip Sidney's
An Apologie for Poetrie, printed in 1595, which he is likely also
to have known. It has been argued that Shakespeare drew as
well upon a version in William Averell's *A Marvailous Combate
of Contrarieties*. The fable appears in many other places, including some of the books read in Elizabethan schools, and it
is thus possible that Shakespeare may have first encountered it
as a schoolboy.

Shakespeare gives the tale a far more prominent position in
his play than it occupies in Plutarch, where it is one of several
means used to induce the people to return to the city at a time
before the events of Shakespeare's play actually have begun.
Shakespeare relates it to famine rather than to usury, as in
Plutarch, and to the problem of rebellion against authority.

Implicit in the tale is not only the idea of the power of the ruler, but also that of the system of obligations and duties binding the ruler to his people which was equally a part of Tudor political theory, and which Shakespeare expressed in all of his political plays.

Coriolanus often has been condemned for the supposed contempt with which the Plebeians are treated and for the savage and scornful vituperation which they are made to endure from the aristocratic hero. Theatre audiences in France are reported to have rioted when the play was performed. But it is only fair to note that it is the mob which receives Shakespeare's censure, and that as individuals the common people are still lovable. As part of the "fickle, many-headed multitude" they are capable only of disorder and destruction to themselves as well as to the state. This is a common Renaissance attitude, and it is no different from what we may find in Shakespeare's earlier plays. The people have grievances, but their leaders, Sicinius and Brutus, are corrupt and petty men who use the plight of the people for their own selfish ends. They are utterly without redeeming virtues.

ALIENATED MAN

The story of Coriolanus has its origins in the still-barbarous world at the very dawn of Roman civilization. As he comes down through Plutarch he is a loud, boisterous soldier, able to frighten the enemy with the very sound of his voice, notable for his great strength and courage and for his scorn for the gentler values and graces which we associate with civilized society. He is passionate, obstinate, and quick to anger, "so choleric and impatient that he would yield to no living creature, which made him churlish, uncivil, and altogether unfit for any man's conversation." He is honest and unselfish, and he is respected by his fellow Patricians in spite of his many shortcomings, but he is utterly without those qualities of reason, judgment and self-control which Plutarch considered essential to any man who would aspire to a role in government. These defects, particularly the violence of his temper and his lack of judgment, led him to turn against his own country and to bring it to the very brink of destruction. Plutarch had attributed the shortcomings of Coriolanus to lack of proper education and training. He had seen the vices as well as the virtues of Coriolanus — the "natural wit and great heart" which "did marvelously stir up his courage to do and attempt noble acts" — and he had regretted that this "natural wit" should have been wasted by lack of education which prevented his virtues from prevailing. Both those qualities which alienated Coriolanus from his fellows, according to Plutarch, and those which endeared him to them are carried over into Shakespeare's play.

Coriolanus has never been among the most beloved of Shakespeare's tragic heroes, and he has been particularly disliked in periods of strong libertarian sentiment, but the aristocratic ideal which he represents is one which Shakespeare's contemporary audience could well understand, and the sentiments which Coriolanus utters — whether or not Shakespeare endorses them — must often have been expressed as well by Jacobean noblemen. Shakespeare does not deny the aristocratic virtues, and they are very real ones, but implicit in the play is the notion that the pursuit of aristocratic ideals may lead to a man's isolation from the rest of humanity. It is this notion which Shakespeare appears to substitute for Plutarch's stress on lack of proper training. Coriolanus exalts honour and public service to the point where their pursuit must be at the expense of those natural human feelings which link man to man without regard to social rank. Out of the very aristocratic qualities which make him noble and magnificent springs the alienation of Coriolanus from his fellow men. This causes them to banish him and causes him at last to reject the bonds of country, family, and friends.

Coriolanus is always alone, as his great victory at Corioli serves to emphasize. He would "stand/ As if a man were author of himself/ And knew no other kin" (V.iii.35–7). Pride, as it was conceived of in theological terms, as the worst of the medieval seven deadly sins, involved a denial of the supremacy of God and thus of one's own brotherhood with his fellow men. It is to such a state that Coriolanus is finally led by his heightened aristocratic awareness of the qualities which separate him from humanity at large. He may be a great solitary fighter, but he can never be a leader of men like Shakespeare's Henry V or Antony, who are bound to their soldiers by ties of love.

For one like Coriolanus, incapable of real relation with his fellow men, to aspire to a role of political leadership is folly, and by this folly he is destroyed. The price of the consulship is to "ask it kindly" (II.III.69) — that is, as a fellow human being, without regard to his aristocratic separation from those he would govern. This Coriolanus cannot do.

There is, nevertheless, in spite of his pride, a tender quality in Coriolanus, an almost childlike simplicity, which appears notably in his relations with his fellow Patricians and particularly with his intimate family. It is finally the mute appeal of his young child, seconding the appeal of Volumnia as she silently holds his hand, which causes him to spare Rome and which leads to his own destruction. Coriolanus is crushed by a tragic conflict between an aristocratic code of honour and the natural demands of ordinary human feeling from which at last he cannot free himself. This conflict brings him to an impasse from which there is no escape, and he dies as he has lived, fighting bravely and hurling defiance at his foes.

VOLUMNIA

Plutarch had reported that Coriolanus had been reared by a widowed mother, had continued to live with her after his own marriage, and had devoted much of his efforts to pleasing her. Plutarch's eloquent description of the hero's tearful yielding to this mother's plea may well have been what most intrigued Shakespeare and drew him to the story, for it is the climactic scene towards which his entire drama builds. But Shakespeare developed the relationship between mother and son far beyond anything in his source. Some critics have seen the hero's tragedy as resulting from a childlike dependence upon his mother and from his final inability to sever the "silver cord" relationship. That Coriolanus lacks the wisdom of maturity is obvious, but to make him a servile "mama's boy" shifts the focus of the play from son to mother and greatly oversimplifies its tragic conflicts.

Volumnia is used for various purposes in Coriolanus. From

her the hero has derived both his heroic grandeur and his aristocratic pride, and one of her functions is to point up both
these aspects of her son. There is a laudable patriotism in her
wish to see him dead in the service of his country rather than
dishonoured by staying out of battle, but there is implicit in it
also a denial of the normal feelings of motherhood which shocks
the contrasting gentle wife, Virgilia. When Coriolanus seeks the
consulship, Volumnia is used both to urge upon him a political
role of which he is inherently incapable and to point out the
political folly of his actions. When she stands before her son in
the final act and pleads for Rome, she becomes the embodiment
of those natural human feelings which Coriolanus at last cannot deny within himself. It has sometimes been observed that
her various roles within the play are not entirely compatible
with one another, but it is with Coriolanus himself that Shakespeare's great concern in this play lies, and minor characters,
though strikingly conceived, are used primarily for the light
they may throw upon the central figure.

THE TRAGEDY OF
Coriolanus

[Dramatis Personæ.

CAIUS MARCIUS, *afterwards* CAIUS MARCIUS CORIOLANUS.
TITUS LARTIUS,
COMINIUS, } *Generals against the Volscians.*
MENENIUS AGRIPPA, *friend to* CORIOLANUS.
SICINIUS VELUTUS,
JUNIUS BRUTUS, } *Tribunes of the People.*
YOUNG MARCIUS, *son to* CORIOLANUS.
A Roman Herald.
NICANOR, *a Roman.*
TULLUS AUFIDIUS, *General of the Volscians.*
Lieutenant to AUFIDIUS.
Conspirators with AUFIDIUS.
ADRIAN, *a Volscian.*
A Citizen of Antium.
Two Volscian Guards.

VOLUMNIA, *mother to* CORIOLANUS.
VIRGILIA, *wife to* CORIOLANUS.
VALERIA, *friend to* VIRGILIA.
Gentlewoman, attending on VIRGILIA.

Senators (Roman and Volscian), Patricians, Ædiles, Lictors, Soldiers, Citizens, Messengers, Servants to Aufidius, Attendants.

SCENE. — *Rome and the neighbourhood; Corioles (Corioli) and the neighbourhood; Antium.*]

Act One

<><><><><><><><><><><><><><><><><><><><><><><><><>

SCENE I. [*Rome. A Street.*]

*Enter a company of mutinous Citizens, with staves,
clubs, and other weapons.*

1. CIT. Before we proceed any further, hear me speak.

ALL. Speak, speak!

1. CIT. You are all resolv'd rather to die than to famish?

ALL. Resolv'd, resolv'd!

1. CIT. First, you know Caius Marcius is chief enemy to the peo- 5
ple.

ALL. We know't, we know't!

1. CIT. Let us kill him, and we'll have corn at our own price. Is't
a verdict?

ALL. No more talking on't! Let it be done! Away, away! 10

2. CIT. One word, good citizens.

1. CIT. We are accounted poor citizens, the patricians good.
What authority surfeits on would relieve us. If they
would yield us but the superfluity while it were wholesome, we might guess they relieved us humanely; but 15
they think we are too dear. The leanness that afflicts us,

I.i. 8 *corn* grain.   9 *a verdict* an agreement.   13 *surfeits* overeats.   *on* F³; F¹:
"one."   14 *yield . . . superfluity* grant us the excess, what they do not need.
14–15 *while it were wholesome* before it rotted (with the implication that it in-
evitably must).   16 *are too dear* would cost (if we were given the excess grain)
more than we are worth.

1

the object of our misery, is as an inventory to particular-
ize their abundance; our sufferance is a gain to them. Let
us revenge this with our pikes ere we become rakes; for
the gods know I speak this in hunger for bread, not in 20
thirst for revenge.

2. CIT. Would you proceed especially against Caius Marcius?

1. CIT. Against him first. He's a very dog to the commonalty.

2. CIT. Consider you what services he has done for his country?

1. CIT. Very well, and could be content to give him good report 25
for't but that he pays himself with being proud.

2. CIT. Nay, but speak not maliciously.

1. CIT. I say unto you, what he hath done famously, he did it to
that end. Though soft-conscienc'd men can be content to
say it was for his country, he did it to please his mother 30
and to be partly proud, which he is, even to the altitude
of his virtue.

2. CIT. What he cannot help in his nature, you account a vice in
him. You must in no way say he is covetous.

1. CIT. If I must not, I need not be barren of accusations. He 35
hath faults (with surplus) to tire in repetition.

Shouts within.

What shouts are these? The other side o' th' city is risen.
Why stay we prating here? To th' Capitol!

ALL. Come, come!

1. CIT. Soft! who comes here?
40

Enter Menenius Agrippa.

---

17 *object* spectacle.   17–18 *an inventory . . . abundance* a catalogue (of human
miseries) which points out to them their own prosperity — they feel their own
wealth more keenly by observing our poverty.   18 *sufferance* suffering.   19 *pikes*
pitch-forks.   *rakes* as lean as rakes.   23 *commonalty* common people.   27 *Nay
. . . maliciously* MALONE; F¹ gives the line to "All."   30–1 *to please . . . partly
proud* partly to please his mother and partly out of pride.   31–2 *altitude of his
virtue* height of his valour. His pride is as high as his valour.   38 *prating* talking
idly.   44 *in hand* in progress, taking place.   46–9 *Our business . . . arms too*
CAPELL; F¹, K give this and the speech beginning at line 67 to Second Citizen. But
Second Citizen has been arguing for reconciliation, and the present arrangement

2. CIT. Worthy Menenius Agrippa, one that hath always lov'd
the people.

1. CIT. He's one honest enough. Would all the rest were so!

MEN. What work 's, my countrymen, in hand? Where go you
With bats and clubs? The matter? Speak, I pray you.   45

1. CIT. Our business is not unknown to th' Senate. They have
had inkling this fortnight what we intend to do, which
now we'll show 'em in deeds. They say poor suitors have
strong breaths; they shall know we have strong arms too.

MEN. Why, masters, my good friends, mine honest neighbours,   50
Will you undo yourselves?

2. CIT. We cannot, sir; we are undone already.

MEN. I tell you, friends, most charitable care
Have the patricians of you. For your wants,
Your suffering in this dearth, you may as well   55
Strike at the heaven with your staves as lift them
Against the Roman state; whose course will on
The way it takes, cracking ten thousand curbs
Of more strong link asunder than can ever
Appear in your impediment. For the dearth,   60
The gods, not the patricians, make it, and
Your knees to them (not arms) must help. Alack!
You are transported by calamity
Thither where more attends you; and you slander
The helms o' th' state, who care for you like fathers,   65
When you curse them as enemies.

1. CIT. Care for us? True indeed! They ne'er car'd for us yet:
suffer us to famish, and their storehouses cramm'd with

---

is accepted by all recent editors.   48 *suitors* petitioners.   49 *strong breaths* (a)
powerful voices (b) stinking breaths — a supposed characteristic of the lower
classes.   51 *undo* ruin.   55 *dearth* famine.   57–60 *whose course . . . your impediment* which will continue in its chosen course, breaking down ten thousand
obstacles, far stronger than any impediments you can offer.   63 *transported*
carried away.   64 *more attends you* more (calamity) is in store for you. He means
open rebellion against the state, which can only increase the difficulties of the
poor.   65 *helms* pilots — i.e. the Patricians who govern.   68 *suffer us to famish*
permit us to starve.

grain; make edicts for usury, to support usurers; repeal
daily any wholesome act established against the rich, and   70
provide more piercing statutes daily to chain up and restrain the poor. If the wars eat us not up, they will; and
there's all the love they bear us.

MEN.   Either you must
Confess yourselves wondrous malicious   75
Or be accus'd of folly. I shall tell you
A pretty tale. It may be you have heard it;
But since it serves my purpose, I will venture
To stale't a little more.

2. CIT.   Well, I'll hear it, sir; yet you must not think to fob off 80
our disgrace with a tale. But, an't please you, deliver.

MEN.   There was a time when all the body's members
Rebell'd against the belly; thus accus'd it:
That only like a gulf it did remain
I' th' midst o' th' body, idle and unactive,   85
Still cupboarding the viand, never bearing
Like labour with the rest; where th' other instruments
Did see and hear, devise, instruct, walk, feel,
And, mutually participate, did minister
Unto the appetite and affection common   90
Of the whole body. The belly answer'd.

2. CIT.   Well, sir, what answer made the belly?

MEN.   Sir, I shall tell you. With a kind of smile,
Which ne'er came from the lungs, but even thus —
For look you, I may make the belly smile   95
As well as speak — it tauntingly replied
To th' discontented members, the mutinous parts
That envied his receipt; even so most fitly

---

71 *piercing* biting, oppressive.   79 *stale't* make it stale, render it trite by retelling
(THEOBALD; F¹: "scale't").   80 *fob off* put off by trickery.   81 *deliver* tell your
tale.   82 *members* parts, organs.   84 *gulf* whirlpool (since it swallows all that
comes within it).   86 *Still* always.   *cupboarding* stowing away.   *viand* food.
87 *Like* similar.   *instruments* organs.   89 *mutually participate* in mutual partnership, working together.   90 *affection* desire.   94 *lungs* These would produce
a hearty laugh, not the kind of sly smile to which Menenius refers.   96 *tauntingly*

As you malign our senators for that
They are not such as you.

2. CIT.   Your belly's answer? What?   100
The kingly crowned head, the vigilant eye,
The counsellor heart, the arm our soldier,
Our steed the leg, the tongue our trumpeter,
With other muniments and petty helps
In this our fabric, if that they —

MEN.   What then?   105
Fore me, this fellow speaks! What then? What then?

2. CIT.   Should by the cormorant belly be restrain'd,
Who is the sink o' th' body —

MEN.   Well, what then?

2. CIT.   The former agents, if they did complain,
What could the belly answer?

MEN.   I will tell you;   110
If you'll bestow a small (of what you have little)
Patience awhile, you'st hear the belly's answer.

2. CIT.   Y'are long about it.

MEN.   Note me this, good friend:
Your most grave belly was deliberate,
Not rash like his accusers, and thus answer'd: 115
"True is it, my incorporate friends," quoth he,
"That I receive the general food at first
Which you do live upon; and fit it is,
Because I am the storehouse and the shop
Of the whole body. But, if you do remember,   120
I send it through the rivers of your blood
Even to the court, the heart, to th' seat o' th' brain,

F⁴; F¹: "taintingly."   98 *his receipt* what he received.   99 *for that* because.
102 *counsellor heart* The heart was considered the organ of understanding; thus
it would give counsel.   104 *muniments* fortifications, defences. *petty helps* minor
supports.   106 *Fore me* a mild oath.   107 *cormorant* rapacious, grasping. The
cormorant is a sea bird noted for its greed.   114 *deliberate* slow and thoughtful
in speech.   116 *incorporate* belonging to a single body.   117 *general* that which
belongs to all.

And, through the cranks and offices of man,
The strongest nerves and small inferior veins
From me receive that natural competency   125
Whereby they live. And though that all at once
You, my good friends" — This says the belly. Mark me.

2. CIT.   Ay, sir, well, well.

MEN.   "Though all at once cannot
See what I do deliver out to each,
Yet I can make my audit up, that all   130
From me do back receive the flour of all
And leave me but the bran." What say you to't?

2. CIT.   It was an answer. How apply you this?

MEN.   The senators of Rome are this good belly,
And you the mutinous members. For, examine   135
Their counsels and their cares, digest things rightly
Touching the weal o' th' common, you shall find
No public benefit which you receive
But it proceeds or comes from them to you,
And no way from yourselves. What do you think,   140
You, the great toe of this assembly?

2. CIT.   I the great toe? Why the great toe?

MEN.   For that, being one o' th' lowest, basest, poorest
Of this most wise rebellion, thou goest foremost.
Thou rascal, that art worst in blood to run,   145
Lead'st first to win some vantage.
But make you ready your stiff bats and clubs.
Rome and her rats are at the point of battle;

---

123 *cranks* winding passages. *offices* work-rooms (literally, those rooms in a
castle where the household work was performed).   124 *nerves* sinews.   125 *competency* adequate portion.   136 *disgest* digest, consider.   137 *weal o' th' common*
welfare of the common people.   143 *For that* because.   145 *rascal* skinny deer,
not worth the trouble of hunting. *worst . . . run* in the poorest condition for
running. To be "in blood" was a hunting term meaning to be "in good condition."   146 *Lead'st first* takes the lead. *win some vantage* gain some personal
advantage.   147 *stiff bats* stout cudgels.   149 *have bale* suffer destruction.
150 *dissentious* rebellious.   151-2 *rubbing . . . scabs* The opinions of the rabble
are regarded by Coriolanus as insignificant nuisances (mere itches) which may be
irritated by them into really troublesome sores. *scabs* (a) sores (b) scurvy creatures.

The one side must have bale.

Enter Caius Marcius.

Hail, noble Marcius!

MAR. Thanks. What's the matter, you dissentious rogues   150
       That, rubbing the poor itch of your opinion,
       Make yourselves scabs?

2. CIT.   We have ever your good word.

MAR. He that will give good words to thee will flatter
       Beneath abhorring. What would you have, you curs,
       That like nor peace nor war? The one affrights you,   155
       The other makes you proud. He that trusts to you,
       Where he should find you lions, finds you hares;
       Where foxes, geese. You are no surer, no,
       Than is the coal of fire upon the ice
       Or hailstone in the sun. Your virtue is   160
       To make him worthy whose offence subdues him,
       And curse that justice did it. Who deserves greatness
       Deserves your hate; and your affections are
       A sick man's appetite, who desires most that
       Which would increase his evil. He that depends   165
       Upon your favours swims with fins of lead
       And hews down oaks with rushes. Hang ye! Trust ye?
       With every minute you do change a mind
       And call him noble that was now your hate,
       Him vile that was your garland. What's the matter   170
       That in these several places of the city
       You cry against the noble Senate, who

---

154 *Beneath abhorring* beyond mere "disgust."   155 *The one* war.   156 *The other* peace.   158 *no surer* no more dependable (THEOBALD; F¹: "surer").   160 *Your virtue* what you consider to be true nobility.   161 *To make . . . subdues him* to bestow honour and esteem upon that man whose deeds degrade him and should subject him to punishment instead.   162 *that justice* that justice which. 162-3 *Who deserves . . . hate* he who merits honour you repay with hatred. 163 *affections* feelings, desires.   165 *evil* sickness. The rabble only desire, he is saying, that which will do them harm.   167 *rushes* reeds, traditionally symbolic of weakness.   169 *your hate* the object of your hatred.   170 *your garland* whom you regard as meriting the highest possible praise.

       (Under the gods) keep you in awe, which else
       Would feed on one another? What's their seeking?

MEN.   For corn at their own rates, whereof they say   175
       The city is well stor'd.

MAR.   Hang 'em! They say?

       They'll sit by th' fire and presume to know
       What's done i' th' Capitol, who's like to rise,
       Who thrives and who declines; side factions and give out
       Conjectural marriages, making parties strong   180
       And feebling such as stand not in their liking
       Below their cobbled shoes. They say there's grain enough?
       Would the nobility lay aside their ruth
       And let me use my sword, I'd make a quarry
       With thousands of these quarter'd slaves as high   185
       As I could pick my lance.

MEN.   Nay, these are almost thoroughly persuaded;
       For though abundantly they lack discretion,
       Yet are they passing cowardly. But I beseech you,
       What says the other troop?

MAR.   They are dissolv'd. Hang 'em!   190
       They said they were anhungry; sigh'd forth proverbs —
       That hunger broke stone walls, that dogs must eat,
       That meat was made for mouths, that the gods sent not
       Corn for the rich men only. With these shreds
       They vented their complainings; which being answer'd   195
       And a petition granted them, a strange one,
       To break the heart of generosity
       And make bold power look pale, they threw their caps
       As they would hang them on the horns o' th' moon,

---

173 *awe* fearful obedience. *which else* who otherwise. 174 *seeking* petition. 178 *like* likely. 179 *side* take sides with. 180 *making parties* calling some factions. 181–2 *feebling . . . shoes* calling those (factions) which they do not like weak, as though they were dirt beneath their mended (cobbled) shoes. 183 *ruth* pity. 184 *quarry* pile of bodies (literally, those of the slain deer at the end of a hunt). 185 *quarter'd* cut into four parts by his sword (as the bodies of hanged criminals were cut). 186 *pick* pitch, throw. 189 *passing* exceedingly. 191 *anhungry* hungry (a variant of "a-hungry"). 194 *shreds* scraps (of proverbial wisdom). 195 *vented* gave expression to, mouthed. *complainings* grievances.

Shouting their emulation.

MEN.   What is granted them?   200

MAR.   Five tribunes to defend their vulgar wisdoms
Of their own choice. One's Junius Brutus,
Sicinius Velutus, and I know not — 'Sdeath!
The rabble should have first unroof'd the city
Ere so prevail'd with me. It will in time   205
Win upon power and throw forth greater themes
For insurrection's arguing.

MEN.   This is strange.

MAR.   Go get you home, you fragments!

Enter a Messenger *hastily.*

MESS.   Where's Caius Marcius?

MAR.   Here. What's the matter?

MESS.   The news is, sir, the Volsces are in arms.   210

MAR.   I am glad on't. Then we shall ha' means to vent
Our musty superfluity. See, our best elders.

Enter Cominius, Titus Lartius, *with
other* Senators; Sicinius Velutus, Junius Brutus.

1. SEN.   Marcius, 'tis true that you have lately told us:
The Volsces are in arms.

MAR.   They have a leader,
Tullus Aufidius, that will put you to't.   215
I sin in envying his nobility;
And were I anything but what I am,
I would wish me only he.

---

answer'd properly met (not merely "replied to").   197 *generosity* the nobility.
200 *Shouting* POPE; F¹: "Shooting."   *their emulation* (a) their rivalry with one
another, each trying to shout louder than the others (b) their malicious envy — of
their superiors.   203 *'Sdeath* by God's death.   204 *unroof'd* THEOBALD; F¹:
"unroo'st."   206 *Win upon power* gain advantage over those in power.   206–7
greater themes . . . arguing greater subjects to be fought over by rebellion.
207 *strange* unnatural.   208 *fragments* mere nothings (a term of contempt).
211 *vent* get rid of.   212 *musty superfluity* stale (worthless) excess population.
215 *to't* to the test.

COM.   You have fought together?

MAR.   Were half to half the world by th' ears, and he
        Upon my party, I'd revolt, to make   220
        Only my wars with him. He is a lion
        That I am proud to hunt.

1. SEN.   Then, worthy Marcius,
        Attend upon Cominius to these wars.

COM.   It is your former promise.

MAR.   Sir, it is,
        And I am constant. Titus Lartius, thou   225
        Shalt see me once more strike at Tullus' face.
        What, art thou stiff? Stand'st out?

TIT.   No, Caius Marcius.
        I'll lean upon one crutch and fight with t'other
        Ere stay behind this business.

MEN.   O, true-bred!

1. SEN. Your company to th' Capitol, where I know   230
         Our greatest friends attend us.

TIT.   [*to* Cominius]   Lead you on.
         [*To* Marcius] Follow Cominius. We must follow you;
         Right worthy you priority.

COM.   Noble Marcius!

1. SEN. [*to the* Citizens] Hence to your homes! be gone!

MAR.   Nay, let them follow.
         The Volsces have much corn. Take these rats thither   235
         To gnaw their garners. Worshipful mutiners,
         Your valour puts well forth. Pray follow.

---

219 *by th' ears* in physical conflict.   220 *Upon my party* on my side.   221 *with him* against him. For Marcius the quality of his adversary is apparently more important than the cause for which he fights.   223 *Attend upon* serve under. 225 *constant* firm (in keeping my promise).   227 *stiff* with age. *Stand'st out* are you staying out (of this war)?   229 *true-bred* really noble.   231 *attend* await. 233 *Right . . . priority* you being well-deserving of the right to go first.   236 *garners* granaries.   237 *puts well forth* displays itself finely (literally, puts forth fair blossoms).   242 *gird* taunt.   243 *modest moon* Since Diana is goddess of

Exeunt. Citizens *steal away. Manent*
Sicinius *and* Brutus.

SIC. Was ever man so proud as is this Marcius?

BRU. He has no equal.

SIC. When we were chosen tribunes for the people — 240

BRU. Mark'd you his lip and eyes?

SIC.   Nay, but his taunts!

BRU. Being mov'd, he will not spare to gird the gods.

SIC. Bemock the modest moon.

BRU. The present wars devour him! He is grown
Too proud to be so valiant.

SIC.   Such a nature, 245
Tickled with good success, disdains the shadow
Which he treads on at noon. But I do wonder
His insolence can brook to be commanded
Under Cominius.

BRU.   Fame, at the which he aims,
In whom already he's well grac'd, cannot 250
Better be held nor more attain'd than by
A place below the first; for what miscarries
Shall be the general's fault, though he perform
To th' utmost of a man, and giddy censure
Will then cry out of Marcius, "O, if he 255
Had borne the business!"

SIC.   Besides, if things go well,
Opinion, that so sticks on Marcius, shall
Of his demerits rob Cominius.

BRU.   Come.

---

virginity as well as of the moon, the moon is modest. 244-5 *He is grown . . .
valiant* his valour (in the wars) has made him too proud. 246 *Tickled with good
success* excited and made eager by good fortune. The metaphor is from the
"tickling" of trout. 246-7 *disdains . . . at noon* scorns the very earth he walks
on. Since the sun is vertical at noon a walker at that time treads on his own
shadow. 248 *brook* endure. 250 *In whom* in which 254 *giddy censure* thought-
less opinion (that of the common people). 258 *demerits* merits, deserts.

Half all Cominius' honours are to Marcius,
Though Marcius earn'd them not; and all his faults   260
To Marcius shall be honours, though indeed
In aught he merit not.

SIC.   Let's hence and hear
How the dispatch is made and in what fashion,
More than his singularity, he goes
Upon this present action.

BRU.   Let's along.   *Exeunt.* 265

❖❖❖❖❖❖❖❖❖❖❖❖❖❖

[SCENE II. *Corioles. The Senate House.*]

Enter Tullus Aufidius *with* Senators *of Corioles.*

1. SEN.   So, your opinion is, Aufidius,
That they of Rome are ent'red in our counsels
And know how we proceed.

AUF.   Is it not yours?
What ever have been thought on in this state
That could be brought to bodily act ere Rome   5
Had circumvention? 'Tis not four days gone
Since I heard thence. These are the words. I think
I have the letter here. Yes, here it is:
"They have press'd a power, but it is not known
Whether for east or west. The dearth is great,   10
The people mutinous; and it is rumour'd,
Cominius, Marcius your old enemy
(Who is of Rome worse hated than of you),

---

259 *are to* belong to.   263 *dispatch is made* business is concluded.   264 *More*
. . . singularity aside from his usual special manner of conducting himself.
    I.II. 2 *are ent'red in our counsels* have become informed of our plans.   3 *yours*
your opinion.   4 *on* F³; F¹: "one."   6 *circumvention* the power to circumvent
(by prior warning). *gone* ago.   9 *press'd a power* impressed (drafted) an army.
13 *of Rome* by the people of Rome.   15 *preparation* army which has been
prepared.   16 *Whither 'tis bent* toward whatever destination it is directed.   19

And Titus Lartius, a most valiant Roman,
These three lead on this preparation   15
Whither 'tis bent. Most likely 'tis for you.
Consider of it."

1. SEN.   Our army 's in the field.
We never yet made doubt but Rome was ready
To answer us.

AUF.   Nor did you think it folly
To keep your great pretences veil'd till when   20
They needs must show themselves, which in the hatching,
It seem'd, appear'd to Rome. By the discovery
We shall be short'ned in our aim, which was
To take in many towns ere (almost) Rome
Should know we were afoot.

2. SEN.   Noble Aufidius,   25
Take your commission; hie you to your bands.
Let us alone to guard Corioles.
If they set down before 's, for the remove
Bring up your army; but, I think, you'll find
Th' have not prepar'd for us.

AUF.   O, doubt not that!   30
I speak from certainties. Nay more,
Some parcels of their power are forth already
And only hitherward. I leave your honours.
If we and Caius Marcius chance to meet,
'Tis sworn between us we shall ever strike   35
Till one can do no more.

ALL.   The gods assist you!

AUF.   And keep your honours safe!

---

answer us meet our attack.   20 pretences plans.   21 in the hatching before they
were fully ripe.   22 appear'd became visible.   23 short'ned in our aim forced
to aim at less than we had intended; made less ambitious in our designs.   24 take
in capture.   26 hie you hasten.   bands companies of soldiers.   28 set down
before's lay siege before our city.   for the remove in order to dislodge them.
32 parcels divisions.   power army.   33 only hitherward coming against us alone
(against no other city).

1. SEN.	Farewell.	
2. SEN.		Farewell.
ALL.	Farewell.	*Exeunt omnes.*

◈◈◈◈◈◈◈◈◈◈◈◈◈◈◈◈

[SCENE III.
Rome. A Room in the house of Marcius.]

Enter Volumnia *and* Virgilia, *mother and wife to* Marcius. *They set them down on two low stools and sew.*

VOL. I pray you, daughter, sing, or express yourself in a more
comfortable sort. If my son were my husband, I should
freelier rejoice in that absence wherein he won honour
than in the embracements of his bed where he would
show most love. When yet he was but tender-bodied and   5
the only son of my womb, when youth with comeliness
pluck'd all gaze his way, when for a day of kings' entreat-
ies a mother should not sell him an hour from her beholding, I (considering how honour would become such
a person; that it was no better than picture-like to hang   10
by th' wall, if renown made it not stir) was pleas'd to let
him seek danger where he was like to find fame. To a
cruel war I sent him, from whence he return'd, his brows
bound with oak. I tell thee, daughter, I sprang not more
in joy at first hearing he was a man-child than now in   15
first seeing he had proved himself a man.

VIR. But had he died in the business, madam, how then?

VOL. Then his good report should have been my son; I therein
would have found issue. Hear me profess sincerely, had

I.III 2 *comfortable sort* cheerful manner.   7 *pluck'd all gaze his way* caused
everyone to look at him (with admiration).   8–9 *from her beholding* out of her
sight.   11 *if renown . . . stir* if desire for fame did not drive it (so honourable a
person) to action.   12 *like* likely.   13–14 *his brows . . . oak* with a garland of
oak leaves on his forehead — the traditional reward for saving the life of a fellow
Roman in battle.   18 *report* reputation.   19 *issue* progeny.   22–3 *voluptuously
surfeit* live in luxurious overindulgence.   27 *hither* coming hither.   31 got

I a dozen sons, each in my love alike, and none less dear   20
than thine and my good Marcius, I had rather had
eleven die nobly for their country than one voluptuously
surfeit out of action.

Enter a Gentlewoman.

GENT.   Madam, the Lady Valeria is come to visit you.

VIR.   Beseech you give me leave to retire myself.   25

VOL.   Indeed you shall not.
Methinks I hear hither your husband's drum;
See him pluck Aufidius down by th' hair;
As children from a bear, the Volsces shunning him.
Methinks I see him stamp thus, and call thus: 30
"Come on, you cowards! You were got in fear,
Though you were born in Rome." His bloody brow
With his mail'd hand then wiping, forth he goes,
Like to a harvestman that's task'd to mow
Or all or lose his hire.   35

VIR.   His bloody brow? O Jupiter, no blood!

VOL.   Away, you fool! It more becomes a man
Than gilt his trophy. The breasts of Hecuba
When she did suckle Hector, look'd not lovelier
Than Hector's forehead when it spit forth blood   40
At Grecian sword, contemning. Tell Valeria
We are fit to bid her welcome.   *Exit* Gentlewoman.

VIR.   Heavens bless my lord from fell Aufidius!

VOL.   He'll beat Aufidius' head below his knee
And tread upon his neck.   45

Enter Valeria (*with an* Usher) *and a*
Gentlewoman.

---

begotten, conceived.   34 *task'd to mow* given the task of mowing.   35 *Or all
. . . hire* either all (the whole field) or lose his salary.   37 *fool* innocent creature.
38 *Than gilt his trophy* than gold becomes his funeral monument. *Hecuba* queen
of Troy, wife of Priam and mother of Hector, the great Trojan hero slain by
Achilles.   41 *contemning* disdaining, holding in contempt.   42 *fit* prepared.
43 *fell* fierce, cruel.

VAL.	My ladies both, good day to you.
VOL.	Sweet madam!
VIR.	I am glad to see your ladyship.
VAL.	How do you both? You are manifest housekeepers. What are you sewing here? A fine spot, in good faith. How 50 does your little son?
VIR.	I thank your ladyship; well, good madam.
VOL.	He had rather see the swords and hear a drum than look upon his schoolmaster.
VAL.	O' my word, the father's son! I'll swear 'tis a very pretty 55 boy. O' my troth, I look'd upon him a Wednesday half an hour together. Has such a confirm'd countenance! I saw him run after a gilded butterfly; and when he caught it, he let it go again, and after it again, and over and over he comes, and up again; catch'd it again; or whether 60 his fall enrag'd him or how 'twas, he did so set his teeth and tear it! O, I warrant, how he mammock'd it!
VOL.	One on 's father's moods.
VAL.	Indeed, la, 'tis a noble child.
VIR.	A crack, madam. 65
VAL.	Come, lay aside your stitchery. I must have you play the idle housewife with me this afternoon.
VIR.	No, good madam. I will not out of doors.
VAL.	Not out of doors?
VOL.	She shall, she shall! 70
VIR.	Indeed, no, by your patience. I'll not over the threshold till my lord return from the wars.
VAL.	Fie, you confine yourself most unreasonably. Come, you

49 *manifest* obvious, well-known. *housekeepers* stay-at-homes. 50 *spot* embroidery pattern. 56 *O' my troth* by my faith. 57 *confirm'd countenance* determined facial expression. 62 *mammock'd it* tore it to pieces. 63 *on 's* of his. 65 *crack* sprightly child, imp. 71 *by your patience* with your permission. 74 *lies in* is expecting a child. 75 *speedy strength* quick recovery. 78 *want* am deficient in. 79 *Penelope* the faithful wife of Ulysses in Homer's ODYSSEY who in her husband's

must go visit the good lady that lies in.

VIR. I will wish her speedy strength and visit her with my   75
      prayers, but I cannot go thither.

VOL. Why, I pray you?

VIR. 'Tis not to save labour nor that I want love.

VAL. You would be another Penelope. Yet, they say, all the
      yarn she spun in Ulysses' absence did but fill Ithaca full   80
      of moths. Come, I would your cambric were sensible as
      your finger, that you might leave pricking it for pity.
      Come, you shall go with us.

VIR. No, good madam, pardon me. Indeed I will not forth.

VAL. In truth, la, go with me, and I'll tell you excellent news   85
      of your husband.

VIR. O, good madam, there can be none yet.

VAL. Verily I do not jest with you. There came news from him
      last night.

VIR. Indeed, madam?   90

VAL. In earnest, it's true; I heard a senator speak it. Thus it is:
      the Volsces have an army forth; against whom Cominius
      the general is gone with one part of our Roman power.
      Your lord and Titus Lartius are set down before their
      city Corioles. They nothing doubt prevailing and to   95
      make it brief wars. This is true, on mine honour; and so
      I pray go with us.

VIR. Give me excuse, good madam. I will obey you in every-
      thing hereafter.

VOL. Let her alone, lady. As she is now, she will but disease   100
      our better mirth.

---

absence devoted herself to weaving.   80 *Ithaca* the island kingdom of Ulysses.
81 *cambric* fine white linen from Cambray in Flanders.   *sensible* capable of
feeling.   82 *leave* stop.   93 *power* army.   94 *set down before* laying siege to.
95 *nothing doubt prevailing* do not at all doubt that they will be victorious.   96
make it brief wars make a short battle of it.   100–1 *disease our better mirth*
cast a pall on our merriment, which would be greater without her.

VAL.   In troth, I think she would. — Fare you well then. —
        Come, good sweet lady. — Prithee, Virgilia, turn thy sol-
        emness out o' door and go along with us.

VIR.   No, at a word, madam. Indeed I must not. I wish you 105
        much mirth.

VAL.   Well then, farewell.   *Exeunt* Ladies.

◇◇◇◇◇◇◇◇◇◇◇◇◇◇◇◇

[SCENE IV. *Before Corioles.*]

Enter Marcius, Titus Lartius, *with* Drum *and* Colours,
    with Captains *and* Soldiers, *as before the City Cori-
    oles: to them a* Messenger.

MAR.   Yonder comes news. A wager they have met.

LART.   My horse to yours, no.

MAR.   'Tis done.

LART.   Agreed.

MAR.   Say, has our general met the enemy?

MESS.   They lie in view, but have not spoke as yet.

LART.   So, the good horse is mine.

MAR.   I'll buy him of you.   5

LART.   No, I'll nor sell nor give him. Lend you him I will
        For half a hundred years. Summon the town.

MAR.   How far off lie these armies?

MESS.   Within this mile and half.

MAR.   Then shall we hear their 'larum and they ours.
        Now, Mars, I prithee make us quick in work,   10

---

105 *at a word* briefly, finally.
    I.IV. 1 *met* encountered in battle.   4 *spoke* encountered.   7 *Summon the
town* call the townsmen to a parley (by sounding the trumpet).   9 *'larum* call to
arms.   12 *fielded friends* comrades on the battlefield.   15 *lesser than a little*
almost not at all.   16 *break* break out of, flee from.   17 *pound* pen, imprison.   18

That we with smoking swords may march from hence
To help our fielded friends! Come, blow thy blast.

> *They sound a parley. Enter two* Sena-
> tors *with others on the walls of Cori-*
> *oles.*

Tullus Aufidius, is he within your walls?

1. SEN. No, nor a man that fears you less than he.
That's lesser than a little.   *Drum afar off.*
                  Hark, our drums   15
Are bringing forth our youth! We'll break our walls
Rather than they shall pound us up. Our gates,
Which yet seem shut, we have but pinn'd with rushes;
They'll open of themselves.   *Alarum far off.*
                Hark you, far off!
There is Aufidius. List what work he makes   20
Amongst your cloven army.

MAR.   O, they are at it!

LART. Their noise be our instruction. Ladders, ho!

> *Enter the* Army *of the* Volsces.

MAR. They fear us not, but issue forth their city.
Now put your shields before your hearts, and fight
With hearts more proof than shields. Advance, brave
    Titus.   25
They do disdain us much beyond our thoughts,
Which makes me sweat with wrath. Come on, my fellows.
He that retires, I'll take him for a Volsce,
And he shall feel mine edge.

> *Alarum. The Romans are beat back to*
> *their trenches. Enter* Marcius, *cursing.*

---

pinn'd with rushes fastened with reeds.   **20** *List* listen.   **21** *cloven* cut up,
divided.   **22** *our instruction* a lesson to us.   **25** *proof* impenetrable.   **26** *beyond*
our thoughts more than we had thought possible.   **28** *retires* retreats.   **29** *edge*
sword.

MAR.   All the contagion of the South light on you,   30
        You shames of Rome! you herd of — Biles and plagues
        Plaster you o'er, that you may be abhorr'd
        Farther than seen and one infect another
        Against the wind a mile! You souls of geese
        That bear the shapes of men, how have you run   35
        From slaves that apes would beat! Pluto and hell!
        All hurt behind! backs red, and faces pale
        With flight and agued fear! Mend and charge home,
        Or, by the fires of heaven, I'll leave the foe
        And make my wars on you! Look to't. Come on!   40
        If you'll stand fast, we'll beat them to their wives,
        As they us to our trenches. Follow me!

                        Another alarum. [*The Volsces retire,*]
                        and Marcius *follows them to gates, and*
                        is shut in.

        So, now the gates are ope. Now prove good seconds.
        'Tis for the followers fortune widens them,
        Not for the fliers. Mark me and do the like.   45
                                        Enter the gates.

1. SOL. Foolhardiness! Not I.

2. SOL.   Nor I.

1. SOL. See, they have shut him in.   *Alarum continues.*

ALL.   To th' pot, I warrant him.

                Enter Titus Lartius.

LART.   What is become of Marcius?

ALL.   Slain, sir, doubtless.

1. SOL. Following the fliers at the very heels,

---

30 *South* The south wind was believed to carry diseases.   31 *Biles* boils (an old
form).   34 *Against . . . mile* so great that the infection will be blown against
the wind for a mile.   36 *Pluto* god of the underworld.   37 *hurt behind* being
wounded as they are fleeing.   38 *agued fear* trembling brought on by fear.
Mend reform your ranks.   *home* to the utmost.   39 *fires of heaven* stars.   42
Follow me K; F¹: "fellowes."   43 *seconds* supporters.   44 *followers* pursuers.
them the gates.   45 *fliers* those who are fleeing.   47 *To th' pot* to his destruction
(a proverbial expression).   51 *Clapp'd to* shut up.   52 *answer* contend against.

With them he enters; who upon the sudden   50
Clapp'd to their gates. He is himself alone,
To answer all the city.

LART.   O noble fellow!
Who sensibly outdares his senseless sword
And when it bows, stand'st up! Thou art lost, Marcius.
A carbuncle entire, as big as thou art,   55
Were not so rich a jewel. Thou wast a soldier
Even to Cato's wish, not fierce and terrible
Only in strokes, but with thy grim looks and
The thunder-like percussion of thy sounds
Thou mad'st thine enemies shake, as if the world   60
Were feverous and did tremble.

> *Enter* Marcius, *bleeding, assaulted by
> the Enemy.*

1. SOL.   Look, sir.

LART.   O, 'tis Marcius!
Let's fetch him off or make remain alike.

> *They fight, and all enter the city.*

◇◇◇◇◇◇◇◇◇◇◇◇◇◇◇◇

[SCENE V. *Corioles. A street.*]

Enter certain Romans *with spoils.*

1. ROM.   This will I carry to Rome.

2. ROM.   And I this.

53–4 *Who sensibly . . . stand'st up* who, being a creature capable of feeling, is
braver than his insensate sword, for he never bows although it does.   54 *lost*
SINGER; F¹: "left," which is retained by some editors.   55 *carbuncle* precious stone.
57 *Cato's* An anachronism. Cato the Censor, who lived long after the time of
Coriolanus, was celebrated as a stoic philosopher and an arbiter of Roman ethics
(THEOBALD; F¹: "Calues").   62 *fetch him off* rescue him.   *make remain alike* stay
to share his fate.

3. ROM.   A murrain on't! I took this for silver.

                    Alarum continues still afar off.

                    Enter Marcius *and* Titus [Lartius]
                    with a Trumpet.

MAR.   See here these movers that do prize their hours
        At a crack'd drachma! Cushions, leaden spoons,   5
        Irons of a doit, doublets that hangmen would
        Bury with those that wore them, these base slaves,
        Ere yet the fight be done, pack up. Down with them!

                            Exeunt [*the* Spoilers].

        And hark, what noise the general makes! To him!
        There is the man of my soul's hate, Aufidius,   10
        Piercing our Romans. Thou, valiant Titus, take
        Convenient numbers to make good the city,
        Whilst I, with those that have the spirit, will haste
        To help Cominius.

LART.   Worthy sir, thou bleed'st.
        Thy exercise hath been too violent for   15
        A second course of fight.

MAR.   Sir, praise me not.
        My work hath yet not warm'd me. Fare you well.
        The blood I drop is rather physical
        Than dangerous to me. To Aufidius thus
        I will appear and fight.

LART.   Now the fair goddess Fortune   20
        Fall deep in love with thee, and her great charms

I.v. 3 *murrain* plague.   4 *movers* cowards, men who will run rather than stand
firm.   *prize their hours* value their time (lives) (F¹; ROWE, K: "honours").   5
drachma Greek coin. Being cracked, it would be worthless.   6 *of a doit* worth a
doit, a small copper coin worth half a farthing.   6–7 *doublets . . . wore them*
The hangman traditionally received the clothes of those he executed as part of
his fee. These doublets (jackets) a hangman would scorn to keep.   12 *Convenient numbers* sufficient troops.   *make good* secure.   15 *exercise* physical
exertion.   16 *course* round. There may be a reference to the "second course" or
"main dish" at a banquet, his previous "exercise" having merely served to whet
his appetite for slaughter.   *praise me not* do not appraise (judge, estimate) my
abilities.   18 *physical* good for the health. Blood-letting was a common means of

Misguide thy opposers' swords! Bold gentleman,
Prosperity be thy page!

MAR.   Thy friend no less
Than those she placeth highest! So farewell.

LART. Thou worthiest Marcius!   [*Exit* Marcius.]   25
.   Go sound thy trumpet in the market place.
       Call thither all the officers o' th' town,
       Where they shall know our mind. Away!   *Exeunt.*

❖❖❖❖❖❖❖❖❖❖❖❖❖❖

[SCENE VI. *Near the camp of* Cominius.]

Enter Cominius *as it were in retire, with* Soldiers.

COM.   Breathe you, my friends. Well fought! We are come off
       Like Romans, neither foolish in our stands
       Nor cowardly in retire. Believe me, sirs,
       We shall be charg'd again. Whiles we have struck,
       By interims and conveying gusts we have heard   5
       The charges of our friends. Ye Roman gods,
       Lead their successes as we wish our own,
       That both our powers, with smiling fronts encount'ring,
       May give you thankful sacrifice!

                Enter a Messenger.

                              Thy news?

MESS.   The citizens of Corioles have issued   10

curing disease.   20-1 *goddess Fortune . . . with thee* Fortune was traditionally
conceived of as a fickle lady but inclined to love the man of valour.   21 *charms*
magical powers (being a goddess).   23 *be thy page* attend thee as a servant.
23-4 *Thy friend . . . highest* may Fortune be no less a friend to you than she
is to those to whom she grants higher rank.

I.VI. 1 *Breathe* rest. *are come off* have left the battle.   3 *retire* withdrawal.
5-6 *By interims . . . our friends* from time to time, carried by the wind, we have
heard the battle noises of our attacking comrades.   7 *Lead their successes* determine what happens to them.   8 *powers* armies. *with . . . encount'ring* meeting one another with smiling faces.   10 *issued* sallied forth.

And given to Lartius and to Marcius battle.
I saw our party to their trenches driven,
And then I came away.

COM.   Thou thou speakest truth,
Methinks thou speak'st not well. How long is't since?

MESS.   Above an hour, my lord.   15

COM.   'Tis not a mile; briefly we heard their drums.
How couldst thou in a mile confound an hour
And bring thy news so late?

MESS.   Spies of the Volsces
Held me in chase, that I was forc'd to wheel
Three or four miles about. Else had I, sir,   20
Half an hour since brought my report.

                 Enter Marcius.

COM.   Who's yonder
That does appear as he were flay'd? O gods!
He has the stamp of Marcius, and I have
Beforetime seen him thus.

MAR.   Come I too late?

COM.   The shepherd knows not thunder from a tabor   25
More than I know the sound of Marcius' tongue
From every meaner man.

MAR.   Come I too late?

COM.   Ay, if you come not in the blood of others,
But mantled in your own.

MAR.   O, let me clip ye
In arms as sound as when I woo'd, in heart   30
As merry as when our nuptial day was done

---

16 *briefly* a little while ago.   17 *confound* waste.   19 *Held me in chase* pursued me. *that* so that.   21 *since* ago.   22 *as he were flay'd* all covered with blood, like a newly skinned carcass hung up in a butcher shop.   23 *stamp* appearance (literally, "impression").   24 *Beforetime* in former times.   25 *tabor* small drum (used by country folk in rural entertainments and morris dances).   27 *From every meaner man* from that of any man of lower social rank.   29 *mantled* clothed, as with a mantle. *clip* embrace.   32 *tapers burn'd to bedward* burning candles (nighttime) summoned us to bed. 34 *decrees* judgment.   36 *Ransoming* releasing after payment of ransom. *pitying* releasing without ransom.   38

And tapers burn'd to bedward!

COM.   Flower of warriors!
How is't with Titus Lartius?

MAR.   As with a man busied about decrees:
Condemning some to death, and some to exile;   35
Ransoming him or pitying, threat'ning th' other;
Holding Corioles in the name of Rome
Even like a fawning greyhound in the leash,
To let him slip at will.

COM.   Where is that slave
Which told me they had beat you to your trenches?   40
Where is he? Call him hither.

MAR.   Let him alone.
He did inform the truth. But for our gentlemen,
The common file (a plague! tribunes for them!),
The mouse ne'er shunn'd the cat as they did budge
From rascals worse than they.

COM.   But how prevail'd you?   45

MAR.   Will the time serve to tell? I do not think.
Where is the enemy? Are you lords o' th' field?
If not, why cease you till you are so?

COM.   Marcius,
We have at disadvantage fought, and did
Retire to win our purpose.   50

MAR.   How lies their battle? Know you on which side
They have plac'd their men of trust?

COM.   As I guess, Marcius,
Their bands i' th' vaward are the Antiates,

---

fawning greyhound Shakespeare habitually associates dogs with subservient flattery.   39 *let him slip* release him.   43 *common file* rank and file, ordinary soldiers (who were usually unwilling conscripts).   44 *budge* flinch, yield in a cowardly fashion.   45 *rascals worse* rogues of even lower social position. A "rascal" was literally "a skinny, worthless deer," and this meaning is also implicit.   51 *battle* army.   52 *men of trust* strongest, most reliable soldiers.   53 *vaward* vanguard.   *Antiates* inhabitants of the city of Antium (POPE; F[1]: "Antients").

Of their best trust; o'er them Aufidius,
Their very heart of hope.

MAR.   I do beseech you,   55
By all the battles wherein we have fought,
By th' blood we have shed together, by th' vows
We have made to endure friends, that you directly
Set me against Aufidius and his Antiates;
And that you not delay the present, but,   60
Filling the air with swords advanc'd and darts,
We prove this very hour.

COM.   Though I could wish
You were conducted to a gentle bath
And balms applied to you, yet dare I never
Deny your asking. Take your choice of those   65
That best can aid your action.

MAR.   Those are they
That most are willing. If any such be here
(As it were sin to doubt) that love this painting
Wherein you see me smear'd; if any fear
Lesser his person than an ill report;   70
If any think brave death outweighs bad life
And that his country 's dearer than himself,
Let him alone, or so many so minded,
Wave thus to express his disposition,
And follow Marcius.   75

They all shout and wave their swords,
take him up in their arms and cast up
their caps.

O, me alone? Make you a sword of me?
If these shows be not outward, which of you

---

58 *endure* continue as.   60 *delay the present* make any delay now.   61 *advanc'd*
raised.   *darts* arrows.   62 *prove* test (our ability as soldiers).   68 *painting* blood.
70 *Lesser* less for (F³; F¹: "Lessen").   *ill report* bad reputation.   71 *think brave*
. . . *life* would rather die bravely than live ignominiously.   73 *so minded* of
similar opinion.   76 *O, me . . . of me* The meaning and the punctuation
of this line have been much debated, and various emendations have been proposed. CAPELL's punctuation is here adopted. It seems to mean "Do you follow
only me (and not the other generals as well)? Do you make me your sword?"   77

But is four Volsces? None of you but is
Able to bear against the great Aufidius
A shield as hard as his. A certain number   80
(Though thanks to all) must I select. The rest
Shall bear the business in some other fight,
As cause will be obey'd. Please you to march;
And four shall quickly draw out my command,
Which men are best inclin'd.

COM.   March on, my fellows.   85
Make good this ostentation, and you shall
Divide in all with us.   *Exeunt.*

◇◇◇◇◇◇◇◇◇◇◇◇◇◇◇◇◇

[SCENE VII. *The gates of Corioles.*]

Titus Lartius, *having set a guard upon* Corioles, *going
with* Drum *and* Trumpet *toward* Cominius *and* Caius
Marcius, *enters with a* Lieutenant, *other* Soldiers,
and a Scout.

LART.   So, let the ports be guarded. Keep your duties
As I have set them down. If I do send, dispatch
Those centuries to our aid; the rest will serve
For a short holding. If we lose the field,
We cannot keep the town.

LIEUT.   Fear not our care, sir.   5

LART.   Hence, and shut your gates upon's.
Our guider, come; to th' Roman camp conduct us.
                                        Exeunt.

---

shows displays, gestures.   *outward* merely external (and thus not indicating true
feeling).   83 *As . . . obey'd* as necessity shall dictate.   84 *four* four officers
(F¹; CAPELL, K: "I").   *draw out my command* select those whom I will lead.   86
ostentation proud showing.   87 *Divide . . . us* share the spoils of battle equally
with us.
    I.VII. 1 *ports* gates.   3 *centuries* companies of a hundred men.   4 *short
holding* endurance of a brief siege.   7 *guider* guide.

◇◇◇◇◇◇◇◇◇◇◇◇◇◇◇◇◇◇

[SCENE VIII.
*A field of battle between the Roman and the
Volscian camp.*]

Alarum, as in battle. Enter Marcius *and* Aufidius *at several doors.*

MAR.   I'll fight with none but thee, for I do hate thee
Worse than a promise-breaker.

AUF.   We hate alike.
Not Afric owns a serpent I abhor
More than thy fame and envy. Fix thy foot.

MAR.   Let the first budger die the other's slave,   5
And the gods doom him after!

AUF.   If I fly, Marcius,
Holloa me like a hare.

MAR.   Within these three hours, Tullus,
Alone I fought in your Corioles walls
And made what work I pleas'd. 'Tis not my blood
Wherein thou seest me mask'd. For thy revenge   10
Wrench up thy power to th' highest.

AUF.   Wert thou the Hector
That was the whip of your bragg'd progeny,
Thou shouldst not scape me here.

                    *Here they fight, and certain Volsces
                    come in the aid of* Aufidius. Marcius

I.VIII. 3 *Not Afric owns* Africa does not possess.   4 *envy* malice. *Fix* place
in position. To fight "foot to foot" was to engage in close personal combat.   5 *the
first budger* he who flinches first.   7 *Holloa . . . hare* hunt me down as the
hunter pursues the hare. The hare was usually symbolic of cowardice.   11
Wrench up raise (with a lever or jack).   12 *whip . . . progeny* the whip used
by your ancestors (progeny), of whom you boast, to scourge their enemies. Hector
was the greatest fighter among the Trojans, who were regarded by the Romans as
their ancestors. Although the syntax is unclear, this is the apparent meaning.
14 *Officious* meddling; offering unwelcome help.   15 *In . . . seconds* by your

> *fights till they be driven in breathless.*

Officious, and not valiant! you have sham'd me
In your condemned seconds.   [*Exeunt.*] 15

❖❖❖❖❖❖❖❖❖❖❖❖❖❖❖❖

[SCENE IX. *The Roman camp.*]

*Flourish. Alarum. A retreat is sounded. Enter, at one
door,* Cominius *with the* Romans; *at another door,*
Marcius, *with his arm in a scarf.*

COM. If I should tell thee o'er this thy day's work,
Thou't not believe thy deeds; but I'll report it
Where senators shall mingle tears with smiles;
Where great patricians shall attend and shrug,
I' th' end admire; where ladies shall be frighted   5
And, gladly quak'd, hear more; where the dull tribunes,
That with the fusty plebeians hate thine honours,
Shall say, against their hearts, "We thank the gods
Our Rome hath such a soldier!"
Yet cam'st thou to a morsel of this feast,   10
Having fully din'd before.

                    Enter Titus [Lartius] *with his* Power,
                    from the pursuit.

LART.   O General,
Here is the steed, we the caparison.
Hadst thou beheld —

MAR.   Pray now, no more. My mother,

---

damned, ineffectual support.
   I.IX. 2 *Thou't* thou wouldst (a common colloquialism).   4 *attend and shrug*
listen and shrug their shoulders (indicating disbelief).   5 *admire* wonder.   6
quak'd terrified, made to tremble.   *dull* (a) stupid (b) sorrowful — at the news.
7 *fusty* mouldy smelling.   8 *against their hearts* unwillingly, in spite of their
true feelings.   10–11 *Yet cam'st . . . din'd before* yet this feast (of victory) was but
a morsel compared to the great dinner (the victory at Corioli) which you had
already eaten.   12 *caparison* trappings of a horse. Coriolanus is the horse; we are
the mere decorations that accompany him.

Who has a charter to extol her blood,
When she does praise me grieves me. I have done   15
As you have done — that's what I can; induc'd
As you have been — that's for my country.
He that has but effected his good will
Hath overta'en mine act.

COM.   You shall not be
The grave of your deserving. Rome must know   20
The value of her own. 'Twere a concealment
Worse than a theft, no less than a traducement,
To hide your doings and to silence that
Which, to the spire and top of praises vouch'd,
Would seem but modest. Therefore, I beseech you   25
(In sign of what you are, not to reward
What you have done) before our army hear me.

MAR.   I have some wounds upon me, and they smart
To hear themselves rememb'red.

COM.   Should they not,
Well might they fester 'gainst ingratitude   30
And tent themselves with death. Of all the horses
(Whereof we have ta'en good, and good store), of all
The treasure in this field achiev'd and city,
We render you the tenth, to be ta'en forth
Before the common distribution at   35
Your only choice.

MAR.   I thank you, General,
But cannot make my heart consent to take

14 *charter . . . blood* special right to praise her own offspring.   18 *effected his good will* accomplished what he had determined to do; done his very best.   19 *overta'en my act* done as much as I.   19–20 *You shall . . . deserving* your merits shall not be buried with you (for lack of recognition by others).   22 *traducement* slander.   24 *to the spire . . . vouch'd* if it were proclaimed (vouch'd) to the greatest height of which praise is capable — like the spires of churches.   26–7 *In sign . . . have done* in recognition of the kind of man you are, and not as payment for what you have done.   29–31 *Should they . . . with death* were they not remembered, they well might fester because of the ingratitude shown them and their only cure be death. A "tent" was a roll of linen inserted into a wound. "To tent" is to cure a wound by probing it with a "tent."   32 *good, and good store* good ones and many of them.   39–40 *stand upon . . . the doing* insist upon taking only my ordinary share (of the spoils) along with all the others who have

A bribe to pay my sword. I do refuse it
And stand upon my common part with those
That have beheld the doing.   40

> *A long flourish. They all cry, "Mar-*
> *cius! Marcius!" cast up their caps and*
> *lances.* Cominius *and* Lartius *stand*
> *bare.*

May these same instruments which you profane
Never sound more! When drums and trumpets shall
I' th' field prove flatterers, let courts and cities be
Made all of false-fac'd soothing! When steel grows
Soft as the parasite's silk, let him be made   45
A coverture for th' wars! No more, I say!
For that I have not wash'd my nose that bled
Or foil'd some debile wretch (which without note
Here's many else have done), you shout me forth
In acclamations hyperbolical,   50
As if I lov'd my little should be dieted
In praises sauc'd with lies.

COM.   Too modest are you,
More cruel to your good report than grateful
To us that give you truly. By your patience,
If 'gainst yourself you be incens'd, we'll put you   55
(Like one that means his proper harm) in manacles,
Then reason safely with you. Therefore be it known,
As to us, to all the world, that Caius Marcius
Wears this war's garland; in token of the which,

---

taken part in the action.   42–4 *When drums . . . soothing* when the instruments
which ordinarily sound the call to battle (drums and trumpets) are used instead
as instruments of flattery, let courts and cities (where flatterers naturally live)
contain nothing but hypocritical flattery.   45–6 *let him . . . th' wars* let it (the
parasite's silk) be used for armour in the wars. *A coverture* TYRWHITT; F¹: "an
Ouerture." The passage has been much debated and much emended. F¹ is obviously corrupt and cannot be made to yield sense without the emendation.   47
For that because.   48 *foil'd* defeated. *debile* feeble. *without note* unnoticed.
49 *shout* F⁴; F¹: "shoot."   50 *acclamations hyperbolical* extravagant and exag-
gerated words of praise.   51 *dieted* fed, sustained.   52 *sauc'd* seasoned.   54
give represent, report.   56 *means* intends. *his proper harm* harm to himself.
59 *garland* wreath of victory.

My noble steed, known to the camp, I give him   60
With all his trim belonging; and from this time,
For what he did before Corioles, call him,
With all th' applause and clamour of the host,
Caius Marcius Coriolanus. Bear
Th' addition nobly ever!   65

Flourish. Trumpets sound and drums.

OMNES.   Caius Marcius Coriolanus!

MAR.   I will go wash;
And when my face is fair, you shall perceive
Whether I blush or no. Howbeit, I thank you.
I mean to stride your steed, and at all times   70
To undercrest your good addition
To th' fairness of my power.

COM.   So, to our tent,
Where, ere we do repose us, we will write
To Rome of our success. You, Titus Lartius,
Must to Corioles back. Send us to Rome   75
The best, with whom we may articulate
For their own good and ours.

LART.   I shall, my lord.

MAR.   The gods begin to mock me. I, that now
Refus'd most princely gifts, am bound to beg
Of my Lord General.

COM.   Take 't; 'tis yours. What is 't?   80

MAR.   I sometime lay here in Corioles
At a poor man's house; he us'd me kindly.
He cried to me; I saw him prisoner;
But then Aufidius was within my view,
And wrath o'erwhelm'd my pity. I request you   85
To give my poor host freedom.

---

61 *trim belonging* trappings that go with him.   64 and 66 *Caius Marcius Coriolanus* ROWE; F¹: "Marcius Caius Coriolanus."   65 *addition* title.   71 *undercrest*
support as though it were a crest (heraldic insignia above a coat of arms).   72
To th' . . . power as becomingly as is in my power.   76 *best* most important
men (of Corioli).   *articulate* come to terms.   79 *bound* obliged.   81 *sometime*

COM.	O, well begg'd!
	Were he the butcher of my son, he should
	Be free as is the wind. Deliver him, Titus.
LART.	Marcius, his name?
MAR.	By Jupiter, forgot!
	I am weary; yea, my memory is tir'd. 90
	Have we no wine here?
COM.	Go we to our tent.
	The blood upon your visage dries; 'tis time
	It should be look'd to. Come. *Exeunt.*

❖❖❖❖❖❖❖❖❖❖❖❖❖

[SCENE X. *The camp of the Volsces.*]

A flourish. Cornets. Enter Tullus Aufidius *bloody, with
two or three* Soldiers.

AUF.	The town is ta'en!
SOLDIER.	'Twill be deliver'd back on good condition.
AUF.	Condition?
	I would I were a Roman; for I cannot,
	Being a Volsce, be that I am. Condition? 5
	What good condition can a treaty find
	I' th' part that is at mercy? Five times, Marcius,
	I have fought with thee. So often hast thou beat me;
	And wouldst do so, I think, should we encounter
	As often as we eat. By th' elements, 10
	If e'er again I meet him beard to beard,
	He's mine, or I am his. Mine emulation
	Hath not that honour in't it had; for where

---

lay at one time lodged.   82 *us'd* treated.   83 *cried* cried out.   88 *Deliver* release.
  I.x. 2 *on good condition* on favourable terms. Aufidius plays on the word in
the sense of "quality."   5 *that* what.   7 *I' th' part . . . mercy* for the side that
is in the power of the victor, dependent on his mercy.   12 *emulation* rivalry,
jealousy.

I thought to crush him in an equal force,
True sword to sword, I'll potch at him some way.   15
Or wrath or craft may get him.

SOLDIER.   He's the devil.

AUF.   Bolder, though not so subtle. My valour 's poison'd
With only suff'ring stain by him; for him
Shall fly out of itself. Nor sleep nor sanctuary,
Being naked, sick, nor fane nor Capitol,   20
The prayers of priests nor times of sacrifice,
Embargements all of fury, shall lift up
Their rotten privilege and custom 'gainst
My hate to Marcius. Where I find him, were it
At home, upon my brother's guard, even there,   25
Against the hospitable canon, would I
Wash my fierce hand in's heart. Go you to th' city.
Learn how 'tis held, and what they are that must
Be hostages for Rome.

SOLDIER.   Will not you go?

AUF.   I am attended at the cypress grove. I pray you   30
('Tis south the city mills) bring me word thither
How the world goes, that to the pace of it
I may spur on my journey.

SOLDIER.   I shall, sir.   [*Exeunt.*]

---

15 *potch* stab, strike.   18 *suff'ring stain* enduring disparagement, eclipse.   19
fly out of itself deviate from its true nature.   20 *fane* temple, religious shrine.
21 *times of sacrifice* holiday seasons.   22 *Embargements* impediments, restraints.
23 *rotten* corrupted by age.   25 *upon . . . guard* under the protection of my
brother.   26 *hospitable canon* law of hospitality.   28 *what* who.   30 *attended*
waited for.   31 *city mills* It has been suggested that Shakespeare may have been
thinking of the four flour mills on the Bankside close to the Globe Theatre. Recol-
lections of his own London often appear in his descriptions of foreign cities.   32–3
that to . . . journey that the rapid movement of events may not leave me behind.

Act Two

◇◇

[SCENE 1. *Rome. A public place.*]

Enter Menenius, *with the two* Tribunes of the People,
Sicinius *and* Brutus.

MEN.   The augurer tells me we shall have news to-night.

BRU.   Good or bad?

MEN.   Not according to the prayer of the people, for they love
not Marcius.

SIC.   Nature teaches beasts to know their friends.   5

MEN.   Pray you, who does the wolf love?

SIC.   The lamb.

MEN.   Ay, to devour him, as the hungry plebeians would the
noble Marcius.

BRU.   He's a lamb indeed, that baes like a bear.   10

MEN.   He's a bear indeed, that lives like a lamb. You two are
old men. Tell me one thing I shall ask you.

BOTH.   Well, sir.

MEN.   In what enormity is Marcius poor in that you two have
not in abundance?   15

BRU.   He's poor in no one fault, but stor'd with all.

II.1 1 *augurer* soothsayer, prophet. He interpreted the meaning of omens.   14
enormity vice.   16 *stor'd* well supplied.

SIC.   Especially in pride.

BRU.   And topping all others in boasting.

MEN.   This is strange now. Do you two know how you are cen-
         sured here in the city, I mean of us o' th' right-hand file?   20
         Do you?

BOTH.   Why, how are we censur'd?

MEN.   Because you talk of pride now — Will you not be angry?

BOTH.   Well, well, sir, well.

MEN.   Why, 'tis no great matter, for a very little thief of occa-   25
         sion will rob you of a great deal of patience. Give your
         dispositions the reins and be angry at your pleasures —
         at the least, if you take it as a pleasure to you in being
         so. You blame Marcius for being proud.

BRU.   We do it not alone, sir.   30

MEN.   I know you can do very little alone; for your helps are
         many, or else your actions would grow wondrous single.
         Your abilities are too infant-like for doing much alone.
         You talk of pride. O that you could turn your eyes to-
         ward the napes of your necks and make but an interior   35
         survey of your good selves! O that you could!

BOTH.   What then, sir?

MEN.   Why, then you should discover a brace of unmeriting,
         proud, violent, testy magistrates (alias fools) as any in
         Rome.   40

SIC.   Menenius, you are known well enough too.

---

20 *o' th' right-hand file* of the superior social classes. "File" is commonly used to
mean "class of persons."   22 *censur'd* judged, estimated.   25-6 *little thief of occasion* slight cause. The "thief" consists of "occasion."   26-7 *Give . . . reins* allow
your natural inclinations to express themselves freely.   27 *at your pleasures* as
you please.   32 *wondrous single* extraordinarily weak.   33 *infant-like* feeble.   38
brace pair. *unmeriting* undeserving.   39 *testy* headstrong, prone to anger.   42
humorous whimsical, governed by humours.   43 *allaying* diluting.   44-5 *imperfect . . . complaint* at fault in tending to take the side of the first complainant in
an argument to state his case.   45 *tinder-like* quick to take fire (become enraged).
trivial motion slight cause.   46 *converses* associates.   46-7 *buttock . . . morning*
tail-end (final hours) of the night, than with the beginning (earliest hours) of
the morning.   48 *spend* get rid of, express. *breath* speech.   149 *wealsmen* politi-

MEN. I am known to be a humorous patrician, and one that
loves a cup of hot wine with not a drop of allaying Tiber
in't; said to be something imperfect in favouring the first
complaint, hasty and tinder-like upon too trivial motion;   45
one that converses more with the buttock of the night
than with the forehead of the morning. What I think, I
utter, and spend my malice in my breath. Meeting two
such wealsmen as you are (I cannot call you Lycurguses),
if the drink you give me touch my palate adversely, I   50
make a crooked face at it. I cannot say your worships
have deliver'd the matter well when I find the ass in com-
pound with the major part of your syllables; and though
I must be content to bear with those that say you are
reverend grave men, yet they lie deadly that tell you have   55
good faces. If you see this in the map of my microcosm,
follows it that I am known well enough too? What harm
can your beesom conspectuities glean out of this character, if I be known well enough too?

BRU. Come, sir, come, we know you well enough.   60

MEN. You know neither me, yourselves, nor anything. You are
ambitious for poor knaves' caps and legs. You wear out a
good wholesome forenoon in hearing a cause between an
orange-wife and a forset-seller, and then rejourn the con-
troversy of threepence to a second day of audience. When   65
you are hearing a matter between party and party, if you
chance to be pinch'd with the colic, you make faces like
mummers, set up the bloody flag against all patience,

---

cians. *Lycurguses* great statesmen. Lycurgus was the great lawgiver of Sparta.
51 *cannot* CAPELL; F¹: "can."   52 *deliver'd* reported, expressed.   52–3 *ass in com-
pound* (a) legal phrases beginning "whereas" (b) stupidity, the signs of the "ass."
54 *bear with* endure.   56 *good* (a) honest (b) handsome.   56 *map* representa-
tion, face. *microcosm* human body (conceived of as a small model of the "macro-
cosm," the physical earth).   58 *beesom* blind. *conspectuities* eyesights.   62 *for
. . . legs* to have poor fellows doff their caps and bow before you.   64 *orange-wife*
woman who sells oranges on the street. *forset-seller* seller of wooden taps for
drawing wine from barrels. A dispute which such a person might have with an
orange-wife, of course, would not be of great importance. *rejourn* adjourn, post-
pone.   65 *day of audience* trial date.   68 *mummers* masqueraders. *set up . . .
against* declare war against, the red flag being a traditional symbol of defiance.

and, in roaring for a chamber pot, dismiss the contro-
versy bleeding, the more entangled by your hearing. All   70
the peace you make in their cause is, calling both the
parties knaves. You are a pair of strange ones.

BRU. Come, come, you are well understood to be a perfecter
giber for the table than a necessary bencher in the Capitol.   75

MEN. Our very priests must become mockers if they shall encounter such ridiculous subjects as you are. When you
speak best unto the purpose, it is not worth the wagging
of your beards; and your beards deserve not so honourable a grave as to stuff a botcher's cushion or to be en- 80
tomb'd in an ass's packsaddle. Yet you must be saying
Marcius is proud; who, in a cheap estimation, is worth
all your predecessors since Deucalion, though peradven-
ture some of the best of 'em were hereditary hangmen.
God-den to your worships. More of your conversation   85
would infect my brain, being the herdsmen of the beastly
plebeians. I will be bold to take my leave of you.

                              Brutus *and* Sicinius *aside*.

                    Enter Volumnia, Virgilia, *and* Valeria.

How now, my as fair as noble ladies — and the moon,
were she earthly, no nobler, whither do you follow your
eyes so fast?   90

VOL. Honourable Menenius, my boy Marcius approaches. For
the love of Juno, let's go.

MEN. Ha? Marcius coming home?

---

70 *bleeding* unhealed. *entangled* confused.   73 *understood* known.   73-4 *perfecter giber . . . bencher* more proficient after-dinner jester than an indispensable
senator.   76 *become mockers* become scoffers (rather than serious judges).   77
subjects creatures.   80 *botcher's cushion* pillow on which a mender of old clothes
traditionally sat.   83 *Deucalion* the Greek equivalent of Noah, who survived a
great flood which wiped out the rest of mankind.   85 *God-den* good evening.
86 *being* since you are.   88 *the moon* Diana, goddess of the moon and of chastity.
Menenius is delicately praising the chastity of the ladies.   89-90 *follow your eyes*
The eyes of the ladies are conceived of as eagerly darting out before them at the
prospect of seeing Coriolanus appear.   94-5 *prosperous approbation* clear evidence

VOL.   Ay, worthy Menenius, and with most prosperous ap-
        probation.   95

MEN.   Take my cap, Jupiter, and I thank thee. Hoo! Marcius
        coming home?

2 LADIES. Nay, 'tis true.

VOL.   Look, here's a letter from him. The state hath another,
        his wife another, and, I think, there's one at home for 100
        you.

MEN.   I will make my very house reel to-night. A letter for me?

VIR.   Yes, certain, there's a letter for you. I saw't.

MEN.   A letter for me? It gives me an estate of seven years'
        health, in which time I will make a lip at the physician. 105
        The most sovereign prescription in Galen is but empiri-
        cutic and, to this preservative, of no better report than a
        horse-drench. Is he not wounded? He was wont to come
        home wounded.

VIR.   O, no, no, no!   110

VOL.   O, he is wounded! I thank the gods for't.

MEN.   So do I too, if it be not too much. Brings 'a victory in his
        pocket? The wounds become him.

VOL.   On's brows. Menenius, he comes the third time home
        with the oaken garland.   115

MEN.   Has he disciplin'd Aufidius soundly?

VOL.   Titus Lartius writes they fought together, but Aufidius
        got off.

MEN.   And 'twas time for him too, I'll warrant him that. An he
        had stay'd by him, I would not have been so fidius'd for 120

---

of great success and honour.   96 *Take my . . . thee* He throws his cap into the
air and offers thanks to the king of the gods.   99 *state* senate.   102 *reel* shake
with joy.   104 *gives me an estate of* endows me with.   105 *make a lip* mock
(with a contemptuous facial expression).   106 *Galen* great medical authority of
ancient Greece.   106–7 *empiricutic* mere quackery.   107 *to this preservative* compared to this medicine. *better report* greater value.   108 *horse-drench* dose of
medicine given to a horse.   115 *the oaken garland* the sign that he has saved the
life of a fellow Roman in battle.   116 *disciplin'd* beaten (like a schoolboy).   120
fidius'd made an Aufidius of.

all the chests in Corioles and the gold that's in them. Is
the Senate possess'd of this?

VOL.   Good ladies, let's go. Yes, yes, yes! The Senate has letters
from the General, wherein he gives my son the whole
name of the war. He hath in this action outdone his for-   125
mer deeds doubly.

VAL.   In troth, there's wondrous things spoke of him.

MEN.   Wondrous? Ay, I warrant you, and not without his true
purchasing.

VIR.   The gods grant them true!   130

VOL.   True? Pow, waw!

MEN.   True? I'll be sworn they are true. Where is he wounded?
[*To the* Tribunes] God save your good worships! Mar-
cius is coming home. He has more cause to be proud. —
Where is he wounded?   135

VOL.   I' th' shoulder and i' th' left arm. There will be large
cicatrices to show the people when he shall stand for his
place. He received in the repulse of Tarquin seven hurts
i' th' body.

MEN.   One i' th' neck, and two i' th' thigh. There's nine that I   140
know.

VOL.   He had before this last expedition twenty-five wounds
upon him.

MEN.   Now it's twenty-seven. Every gash was an enemy's grave.

                                        (*A shout and flourish.*)
Hark! the trumpets.   145

VOL.   These are the ushers of Marcius. Before him he carries
noise, and behind him he leaves tears.
Death, that dark spirit, in's nervy arm doth lie,
Which, being advanc'd, declines, and then men die.

122 *possess'd* informed.   125 *name* credit, glory.   128-9 *true purchasing* honest
earning.   131 *Pow, waw* an expression of contempt, like "pish, pish."   137-8
his place the consulship. Volumnia sees this position as inherently belonging to
her son.   138 *repulse of Tarquin* The first great battle of Coriolanus, according
to Plutarch, had been against Tarquin the Proud, upon his attempt to regain

*A sennet. Trumpets sound. Enter Co-
minius the General and Titus Lartius;
between them, Coriolanus, crown'd
with an oaken garland; with Captains
and Soldiers and a Herald.*

HERALD. Know, Rome, that all alone Marcius did fight   150
Within Corioles gates, where he hath won,
With fame, a name to Caius Marcius. These
In honour follows Coriolanus. Welcome,
Welcome to Rome, renowned Coriolanus!

Sound. Flourish.

ALL.   Welcome to Rome, renowned Coriolanus!   155

COR.   No more of this; it does offend my heart.
Pray now, no more.

COM.   Look, sir, your mother!

COR.   O,
You have, I know, petition'd all the gods
For my prosperity.   *Kneels.*

VOL.   Nay, my good soldier, up.
My gentle Marcius, worthy Caius, and   160
By deed-achieving honour newly nam'd —
What is it — Coriolanus — must I call thee?
But O, thy wife!

COR.   My gracious silence, hail!
Wouldst thou have laugh'd had I come coffin'd home
That weep'st to see me triumph? Ah, my dear,   165
Such eyes the widows in Corioles wear
And mothers that lack sons.

MEN.   Now the gods crown thee!

COR.   And live you yet? [*To* Valeria] O my sweet lady, pardon.

Rome in 499 B.C.   146 *ushers* escorts.   148 *nervy* sinewy, strong.   149 *advanc'd*
raised. *declines* descends.   152 *With* in addition to.   161 *deed-achieving honour*
honour achieved by the performance of deeds.   168 *And live you yet* He is being
jocular with Menenius.

VOL.   I know not where to turn. O, welcome home!
And welcome, General! and y'are welcome all!   170

MEN.   A hundred thousand welcomes! I could weep
And I could laugh; I am light and heavy. Welcome.
A curse begin at very root on's heart
That is not glad to see thee! You are three
That Rome should dote on; yet, by the faith of men,   175
We have some old crabtrees here at home that will not
Be grafted to your relish. Yet welcome, warriors!
We call a nettle but a nettle and
The faults of fools but folly.

COM.   Ever right.

COR.   Menenius, ever, ever.   180

HERALD. Give way there, and go on!

COR.   [*to* Volumnia *and* Virgilia] Your hand, and yours!
Ere in our own house I do shade my head,
The good patricians must be visited,
From whom I have receiv'd not only greetings,
But with them change of honours.

VOL.   I have liv'd   185
To see inherited my very wishes,
And the buildings of my fancy. Only
There's one thing wanting, which I doubt not but
Our Rome will cast upon thee.

COR.   Know, good mother,
I had rather be their servant in my way   190

---

172 *light* merry. *heavy* sad.   173 *begin . . . heart* penetrate to the very bottom of his heart.   176 *old crabtrees* i.e. the tribunes, sour old men.   177 *grafted to your relish* made to like you (literally "have a liking for you grafted to them").   179 *Ever* still.   185 *change of* a variety of — as in "a change of clothes" (F¹; THEOBALD, K: "charge of").   186 *inherited* realized.   187 *the buildings of my fancy* what my dreams have envisaged.   191 *sway* rule.   192–3 *bleared . . . spectacled* those with faulty vision put on spectacles.   194 *rapture* fit of excitement.   195 *chats him* gossips about him.   *Malkin* slattern, wench (a diminutive form of "Maud").   196 *lockram* coarse linen.   *reechy* dirty, greasy.   197 *Stalls* shops. *bulks* shop-fronts.   198 *leads* roofs (covered with lead).   *ridges* roof-edges.   198–9 *hors'd . . . complexions* bearing people of every type. The "complexion" referred literally to the combination of the humours in the body and thus to "per-

Than sway with them in theirs.

COM.   On, to the Capitol!

*Flourish. Cornets. Exeunt in state, as
before.* Brutus *and* Sicinius [*come forward*].

BRU.   All tongues speak of him, and the bleared sights
Are spectacled to see him. Your prattling nurse
Into a rapture lets her baby cry
While she chats him. The kitchen Malkin pins   195
Her richest lockram 'bout her reechy neck,
Clamb'ring the walls to eye him. Stalls, bulks, windows
Are smother'd up, leads fill'd, and ridges hors'd
With variable complexions, all agreeing
In earnestness to see him. Seld-shown flamens   200
Do press among the popular throngs and puff
To win a vulgar station. Our veil'd dames
Commit the war of white and damask in
Their nicely gauded cheeks to th' wanton spoil
Of Phœbus' burning kisses. Such a poother   205
As if that whatsoever god who leads him
Were slily crept into his human powers
And gave him graceful posture.

SIC.   On the sudden
I warrant him consul.

BRU.   Then our office may
During his power go sleep.   210

---

sonality," which was dependent upon this particular combination.   199 *agreeing*
equal.   200 *Seld-shown flamens* sacred priests who are seldom seen.   201–2 *puff
. . . station* exert themselves to gain a position of vantage among the common
people (with whom they ordinarily do not associate).   203 *damask* red.   204
nicely gauded daintily and carefully adorned. *wanton spoil* careless destruction.
205 *Phœbus' burning kisses* the sun's rays. Phœbus, the sun god, being the source
of fertility, is often conceived of as an amorous lover, and thus his kisses are
"wanton" in the sense of "licentious." *poother* pother, confusion.   206–8 *As if
. . . posture* as if his guardian angel has secretly entered into him and given him
the bearing of a god. That man could be guided by a "genius" or special divinity
was an ancient belief among the Romans.

SIC.　He cannot temp'rately transport his honours
　　From where he should begin and end, but will
　　Lose those he hath won.

BRU.　　　　　　　　　In that there's comfort.

SIC.　　　　　　　　　　　　　Doubt not
　　The commoners, for whom we stand, but they
　　Upon their ancient malice will forget　　　　　215
　　With the least cause these his new honours; which
　　That he will give them make I as little question
　　As he is proud to do't.

BRU.　　　　　　　I heard him swear,
　　Were he to stand for consul, never would he
　　Appear i' th' market place, nor on him put　　220
　　The napless vesture of humility,
　　Nor, showing (as the manner is) his wounds
　　To th' people, beg their stinking breaths.

SIC.　　　　　　　　　　'Tis right.

BRU.　It was his word. O, he would miss it, rather
　　Than carry it but by the suit of the gentry to him　　225
　　And the desire of the nobles.

SIC.　　　　　　　I wish no better
　　Than have him hold that purpose and to put it
　　In execution.

BRU.　　　　'Tis most like he will.

SIC.　It shall be to him then, as our good wills,
　　A sure destruction.

BRU.　　　　　　So it must fall out　　230
　　To him or our authorities. For an end,
　　We must suggest the people in what hatred

211–13 *He cannot . . . has won* he cannot conduct himself with sufficient self-control (temp'rately), from beginning to end, so as to keep his honours, and thus he will lose those honours he has won.　215 *Upon* because of.　216 *With the least cause* upon the slightest provocation.　216–8 *which . . . to do't* which provocation I am as certain he will give them as I am certain that his pride will lead him to do it.　221 *napless* worn-out, threadbare (ROWE; F¹: "Naples").　*vesture* garment.　224 *miss it* go without it (the consulship).　225 *carry* win.　227 *hold that purpose* stick to that intention (to stand for consul).　228 *like* likely.　229

He still hath held them; that to's power he would
Have made them mules, silenc'd their pleaders, and
Dispropertied their freedoms; holding them,   235
In human action and capacity,
Of no more soul nor fitness for the world
Than camels in the war, who have their provand
Only for bearing burdens, and sore blows
For sinking under them.

SIC.   This, as you say, suggested   240
At some time when his soaring insolence
Shall touch the people — which time shall not want
If he be put upon't, and that's as easy
As to set dogs on sheep — will be his fire
To kindle their dry stubble; and their blaze   245
Shall darken him for ever.

Enter a Messenger.

BRU.   What's the matter?

MESS.   You are sent for to the Capitol. 'Tis thought
That Marcius shall be consul.
I have seen the dumb men throng to see him and
The blind to hear him speak. Matrons flung gloves,   250
Ladies and maids their scarfs and handkerchers,
Upon him as he pass'd; the nobles bended
As to Jove's statue, and the commons made
A shower and thunder with their caps and shouts.
I never saw the like.

BRU.   Let's to the Capitol,   255
And carry with us ears and eyes for th' time,
But hearts for the event.

SIC.   Have with you.   *Exeunt.*

---

good wills well-being requires.   231 *authorities* offices.   *For an end* in short.   232
suggest insinuate to.   233 *still* always.   234 *mules* beasts of burden, slaves.   235
Dispropertied dispossessed them of.   *holding them* regarding them as.   238 *the
war* HANMER; F¹: "their Warre."   *provand* provender, food.   240 *suggested* insin-
uated (to the people).   242 *touch* deeply affect, move (HANMER; F¹: "teach").
want be lacking.   243 *put upon't* provoked to such behaviour.   246 *darken him*
put out his light.   257 *hearts for the event* courage to endure the outcome.

◇◇◇◇◇◇◇◇◇◇◇◇◇◇◇◇◇◇

[SCENE II. *Rome. The Capitol.*]

Enter two Officers, *to lay cushions, as it were in the*
Capitol.

1. OFF.   Come, come, they are almost here. How many stand for
consulships?

2. OFF.   Three, they say; but 'tis thought of every one Coriolanus
will carry it.

1. OFF.   That's a brave fellow; but he's vengeance proud and   5
loves not the common people.

2. OFF.   Faith, there hath been many great men that have
flatter'd the people, who ne'er loved them; and there be
many that they have loved, they know not wherefore; so
that, if they love they know not why, they hate upon no   10
better a ground. Therefore, for Coriolanus neither to
care whether they love or hate him manifests the true
knowledge he has in their disposition, and out of his
noble carelessness lets them plainly see't.

1. OFF.   If he did not care whether he had their love or no, he   15
waved indifferently 'twixt doing them neither good nor
harm; but he seeks their hate with greater devotion than
they can render it him and leaves nothing undone that
may fully discover him their opposite. Now to seem to
affect the malice and displeasure of the people is as bad   20
as that which he dislikes — to flatter them for their love.

2. OFF.   He hath deserved worthily of his country; and his ascent

---

II.II. 5 *brave* fine. *vengeance proud* proud with a vengeance, exceedingly
proud.   7 *there* F¹; K: "here."   13 *in* of. *out of* because of.   14 *noble careless-*
ness aristocratic indifference (to what the common people think of him).   16
waved would have wavered.   17 *devotion* ardour.   19 *discover . . . opposite*
reveal him to be their enemy.   20 *affect* cultivate.   23 *degrees* steps. *as those* as
the ascent of those.   24 *supple* subservient.   24-6 *bonneted . . . and report*
doffed their hats, and never did anything else, to gain popularity and reputation

is not by such easy degrees as those who, having been
supple and courteous to the people, bonneted, without
any further deed to have them at all into their estima-　25
tion and report; but he hath so planted his honours in
their eyes and his actions in their hearts that for their
tongues to be silent and not confess so much were a kind
of ingrateful injury; to report otherwise were a malice
that, giving itself the lie, would pluck reproof and re-　30
buke from every ear that heard it.

1. OFF.　No more of him; he's a worthy man. Make way; they are
coming.

> A sennet. *Enter the* Patricians *and the*
> Tribunes of the People, Lictors *before*
> *them;* Coriolanus, Menenius, Cominius
> *the* Consul. Sicinius *and* Brutus *take*
> *their places by themselves.* Coriolanus
> *stands.*

MEN.　Having determin'd of the Volsces and
To send for Titus Lartius, it remains,　35
As the main point of this our after-meeting,
To gratify his noble service that
Hath thus stood for his country. Therefore please you,
Most reverend and grave elders, to desire
The present consul and last general　40
In our well-found successes, to report
A little of that worthy work perform'd
By Caius Marcius Coriolanus, whom
We met here both to thank, and to remember
With honours like himself.　　　[Coriolanus *sits.*]

1. SEN.　　　　　　　　Speak, good Cominius.　45

---

with the people.　26–7 *so planted . . . hearts* made them see clear evidence of
his great honours and feel the valour of his actions.　30 *giving . . . lie* revealing
itself as flagrantly untrue.　33 s.d. *Lictors* attendants upon Roman magistrates.
34 *determin'd of* come to a decision about.　36 *after-meeting* meeting following
an earlier meeting.　37 *gratify* reward.　38 *stood for* defended.　39 *desire* request.　41 *well-found* fortunately met with.　43 *Caius Marcius* ROWE; F¹: "Mar-
tius Caius."　44 *remember* memorialize.

Leave nothing out for length, and make us think
Rather our state 's defective for requital
Than we to stretch it out. [*To the* Tribunes] Masters o'
    th' people,
We do request your kindest ears, and after,
Your loving motion toward the common body   50
To yield what passes here.

SIC.   We are convented
Upon a pleasing treaty, and have hearts
Inclinable to honour and advance
The theme of our assembly.

BRU.   Which the rather
We shall be blest to do, if he remember   55
A kinder value of the people than
He hath hereto priz'd them at.

MEN.   That's off, that's off!
I would you rather had been silent. Please you
To hear Cominius speak?

BRU.   Most willingly;
But yet my caution was more pertinent   60
Than the rebuke you give it.

MEN.   He loves your people;
But tie him not to be their bedfellow.
Worthy Cominius, speak.

           Coriolanus *rises, and offers to go away.*

              Nay, keep your place.

1. SEN. Sit, Coriolanus. Never shame to hear
What you have nobly done.

46–8 *make us . . . it out* make us rather believe that our government is too poor
to adequately reward services than that we are unwilling to strain our resources
(stretch it out) for such a purpose.   50 *loving . . . body* kind intercession with
the common people.   51 *yield* grant.   *what passes* what is voted on.   *convented*
summoned, convened.   52 *pleasing treaty* pleasant proposal.   54 *theme of our
assembly* subject of our meeting (Coriolanus).   55 *blest to do* happy to perform.
57 *off* beside the point.   68 *disbench'd you* cause you to leave your seat.   70
sooth'd flattered.   71 *weigh* are valued, have merit.   72–3 *have one . . . struck*

COR.   Your Honours' pardon.   65
   I had rather have my wounds to heal again
   Than hear say how I got them.

BRU.   Sir, I hope
   My words disbench'd you not.

COR.   No, sir. Yet oft,
   When blows have made me stay, I fled from words.
   You sooth'd not, therefore hurt not; but your people,   70
   I love them as they weigh —

MEN.   Pray now, sit down.

COR.   I had rather have one scratch my head i' th' sun
   When the alarum were struck than idly sit
   To hear my nothings monster'd.   *Exit.*

MEN.   Masters of the people,
   Your multiplying spawn how can he flatter   75
   (That's thousand to one good one) when you now see
   He had rather venture all his limbs for honour
   Than one on's ears to hear it? Proceed, Cominius.

COM.   I shall lack voice. The deeds of Coriolanus
   Should not be utter'd feebly. It is held   80
   That valour is the chiefest virtue and
   Most dignifies the haver. If it be,
   The man I speak of cannot in the world
   Be singly counterpois'd. At sixteen years,
   When Tarquin made a head for Rome, he fought   85
   Beyond the mark of others. Our then Dictator,
   Whom with all praise I point at, saw him fight
   When with his Amazonian chin he drove

---

i.e. be idly self-indulgent rather than taking part in a battle.   *alarum* call to
arms.   74 *monster'd* treated as though they were marvels.   75 *multiplying
spawn* common people who reproduce like animals.   76 *That's thousand . . . one*
in which only one in a thousand is of any worth.   78 *on's* of his.   84 *singly
counterpois'd* equalled by any other single person. The metaphor is that of the
balances of a scale.   85 *made a head for* gathered an army against.   86 *mark*
power.   88 *Amazonian chin* fierce but beardless chin. The Amazonians were the
strong female warriors who supposedly lived in Scythia.

The bristled lips before him. He bestrid
An o'erpress'd Roman and i' th' consul's view   90
Slew three opposers. Tarquin's self he met
And struck him on his knee. In that day's feats,
When he might act the woman in the scene,
He prov'd best man i' th' field and for his meed
Was brow-bound with the oak. His pupil age   95
Man-ent'red thus, he waxed like a sea,
And in the brunt of seventeen battles since
He lurch'd all swords of the garland. For this last,
Before and in Corioles, let me say
I cannot speak him home. He stopp'd the fliers   100
And by his rare example made the coward
Turn terror into sport. As weeds before
A vessel under sail, so men obey'd
And fell below his stem. His sword, death's stamp,
Where it did mark, it took. From face to foot   105
He was a thing of blood, whose every motion
Was tim'd with dying cries. Alone he ent'red
The mortal gate of th' city, which he painted
With shunless destiny; aidless came off,
And with a sudden reinforcement struck   110
Corioles like a planet. Now all's his,
When by-and-by the din of war gan pierce
His ready sense; then straight his doubled spirit
Requick'ned what in flesh was fatigate,
And to the battle came he, where he did   115

---

89 *bristled lips* i.e. older men (having moustaches). *bestrid* To "bestride" a
fallen soldier was to stand with one leg on either side of him and with sword
drawn so as to protect him from the foe.   90 *o'erpress'd* overwhelmed (by the
enemy).   93 *When he . . . scene* Being a mere boy, Coriolanus would have more
appropriately acted a woman's than a man's part if the battle were a play.
Women's parts, of course, were taken by boys.   94 *meed* reward.   95 *Was . . .
oak* had the oaken wreath (for rescuing a fellow Roman) placed upon his brow.
96 *Man-ent'red* having been initiated into manhood. *waxed* grew, developed.
97 *brunt* shock.   98 *lurch'd . . . garland* stole (lurch'd) the garland of victory
from all other soldiers.   100 *speak him home* praise him sufficiently. *fliers* those
in retreat.   102 *weeds* F¹; F², κ: "waues." There is nothing unusual about the image of weeds being scattered before the prow of a ship, and thus no reason to depart from the F¹ text.   104 *stem* prow of a ship. *stamp* instrument (literally, the
press used for stamping out coins; his sword is conceived of as producing death

Run reeking o'er the lives of men, as if
'Twere a perpetual spoil; and till we call'd
Both field and city ours, he never stood
To ease his breast with panting.

MEN.   Worthy man!

1. SEN.   He cannot but with measure fit the honours   120
Which we devise him.

COM.   Our spoils he kick'd at
And look'd upon things precious as they were
The common muck of the world. He covets less
Than misery itself would give, rewards
His deeds with doing them, and is content   125
To spend the time to end it.

MEN.   He's right noble.
Let him be call'd for.

1. SEN.   Call Coriolanus.

OFFICER. He doth appear.

Enter Coriolanus.

MEN.   The Senate, Coriolanus, are well pleas'd
To make thee consul.

COR.   I do owe them still   130
My life and services.

MEN.   It then remains
That you do speak to the people.

---

in such a manner).   107 *tim'd* accompanied rhythmically. The cries are conceived
of as the accompanying music to his dancelike "motion."   108 *mortal* deadly.
109 *shunless destiny* blood whose flowing was inevitable. *aidless came off* retired
(from the city) without having been assisted.   111 *like a planet* For a planet to
"strike" a man was for it to destroy him by its malign influence. The term is an
astrological one. *all's his* he is victorious (master of all).   112 *gan* began.   113
ready sense alert sense (of hearing the sounds of battle). *straight* at once. *doubled*
strengthened.   114 *Requick'ned . . . fatigate* revived his weary body.   116 *Run
reeking* Wherever he ran, a hot steam (reek) of blood accompanied him.   117
perpetual spoil endless slaughter.   118 *stood* stopped.   120 *with measure* becomingly.   122 *as they were* as though they were.   124 *misery* wretchedness, poverty. He asks no more gain than the poorest person is capable of giving.   125–6
is content . . . end it is willing to devote whatever time is necessary for him to
accomplish his deeds.   130 *still* always, perpetually.

COR.   I do beseech you,
Let me o'erleap that custom; for I cannot
Put on the gown, stand naked, and entreat them
For my wounds' sake to give their suffrage. Please you   135
That I may pass this doing.

SIC.   Sir, the people
Must have their voices; neither will they bate
One jot of ceremony.

MEN.   Put them not to't.
Pray you go fit you to the custom and
Take to you, as your predecessors have,   140
Your honour with the form.

COR.   It is a part
That I shall blush in acting, and might well
Be taken from the people.

BRU.   [to Sicinius]   Mark you that?

COR.   To brag unto them, "Thus I did, and thus!"
Show them th' unaching scars which I should hide,   145
As if I had receiv'd them for the hire
Of their breath only!

MEN.   Do not stand upon't.
We recommend to you, Tribunes of the People,
Our purpose to them; and to our noble consul
Wish we all joy and honour.   150

1. SEN.   To Coriolanus come all joy and honour!

Flourish. Cornets. Then exeunt. Manent
Sicinius and Brutus.

BRU.   You see how he intends to use the people.

SIC.   May they perceive 's intent! He will require them

---

133 *o'erleap* skip, omit.   134 *naked* unarmed (in civilian clothes).   135 *suffrage*
votes.   137 *voices* votes.   *bate* abate, lessen.   138 *ceremony* formal procedure.
Put incite.   139 *fit you* adapt yourself.   141 *form* formal ceremony.   142 *might
well* it (the custom) might well.   146-7 *for the hire . . . only* merely in order
to buy their votes.   *breath* voice, vote.   147 *stand* insist.   148 *recommend to
you* trust to your good offices.   149 *purpose to them* announcement of our intentions to them (the people).   153-5 *He will . . . to give* he will ask (require)

As if he did contemn what he requested
Should be in them to give.

BRU.   Come, we'll inform them   155
Of our proceedings here. On th' market place
I know they do attend us.   [*Exeunt.*]

❖❖❖❖❖❖❖❖❖❖❖❖❖❖❖

[SCENE III. *Rome. The Forum.*]

Enter seven or eight Citizens.

1. CIT.   Once if he do require our voices, we ought not to deny
           him.

2. CIT.   We may, sir, if we will.

3. CIT.   We have power in ourselves to do it, but it is a power
           that we have no power to do; for if he show us his   5
           wounds and tell us his deeds, we are to put our tongues
           into those wounds and speak for them. So, if he tell us
           his noble deeds, we must also tell him our noble accept-
           ance of them. Ingratitude is monstrous; and for the
           multitude to be ingrateful were to make a monster of   10
           the multitude, of the which we being members, should
           bring ourselves to be monstrous members.

1. CIT.   And to make us no better thought of, a little help will
           serve; for once we stood up about the corn, he himself
           stuck not to call us the many-headed multitude.   15

3. CIT.   We have been call'd so of many; not that our heads
           are some brown, some black, some abram, some bald, but
           that our wits are so diversely colour'd. And truly I think,

them (for their votes) as though he regarded it as contemptible that what he
asked for should be in their power to give.   157 *attend* wait for.
    II.III. 4-5 *We have . . . to do* we have authority to do it, but no moral power or
right to do it.   6-7 *tongues . . . wounds* The conception of wounds as mouths
is a favourite metaphor with Shakespeare.   15 *stuck not* did not hesitate.   *many-
headed multitude* This scornful epithet as applied to the mob is a Renaissance
commonplace.   16 *of* by.   17 *abram* auburn (an old form of the word).

if all our wits were to issue out of one skull, they would
fly east, west, north, south, and their consent of one   20
direct way should be at once to all the points o' th'
compass.

2. CIT.   Think you so? Which way do you judge my wit would
fly?

3. CIT.   Nay, your wit will not so soon out as another man's will.   25
'Tis strongly wedg'd up in a blockhead. But if it were
at liberty, 'twould sure southward.

2. CIT.   Why that way?

3. CIT.   To lose itself in a fog; where being three parts melted
away with rotten dews, the fourth would return for   30
conscience sake, to help to get thee a wife.

2. CIT.   You are never without your tricks. You may, you may!

3. CIT.   Are you all resolv'd to give your voices? But that's no
matter, the greater part carries it. I say, if he would
incline to the people, there was never a worthier man.   35

Enter Coriolanus *in a gown of humility, with* Menenius.

Here he comes, and in the gown of humility. Mark his
behaviour. We are not to stay all together, but to come
by him where he stands, by ones, by twos, and by threes.
He's to make his requests by particulars; wherein every
one of us has a single honour, in giving him our own   40
voices with our own tongues. Therefore follow me, and
I'll direct you how you shall go by him.

ALL.   Content, content!

[*Exeunt* Citizens.]

---

20 *consent of* agreement about.   25 *out* come out.   27 *surely* surely go. *southward* traditionally the region of fog, both fog and rain being carried by the south
wind.   30 *rotten* unwholesome (since fog and rain were believed to carry disease).   31 *get thee a wife* Presumably because he is too stupid to woo one for
himself.   32 *tricks* jokes. *You may* go on (have your joke).   33 *resolv'd* decided.
34 *greater part* majority.   35 *incline to* take the side of.   39 *by particulars* to

MEN.   O sir, you are not right. Have you not known
The worthiest men have done't?

COR.   What must I say?   45
"I pray, sir" — Plague upon't! I cannot bring
My tongue to such a pace. "Look, sir, my wounds.
I got them in my country's service, when
Some certain of your brethren roar'd, and ran
From th' noise of our own drums."

MEN.   O me, the gods!   50
You must not speak of that. You must desire them
To think upon you.

COR.   Think upon me? Hang 'em!
I would they would forget me, like the virtues
Which our divines lose by 'em.

MEN.   You'll mar all.
I'll leave you. Pray you speak to 'em. I pray you,   55
In wholesome manner.   *Exit.*

Enter three of the Citizens.

COR.   Bid them wash their faces
And keep their teeth clean. So, here comes a brace.
You know the cause, sir, of my standing here.

3. CIT.   We do, sir. Tell us what hath brought you to't.

COR.   Mine own desert.   60

2. CIT.   Your own desert?

COR.   Ay, not mine own desire.

3. CIT.   How? Not your own desire?

COR.   No, sir, 'twas never my desire yet to trouble the poor
with begging.   65

---

individuals, one by one.   47 *to such a pace* to such gentle words. The metaphor
is from horsemanship.   51 *desire* request.   52 *think upon* think favourably of.
53–4 *like the . . . by 'em* like the virtues which our preachers are unable to
inculcate in them, and thus waste their labours in the attempt. The expression
is very elliptical, but this seems to be the meaning.   56 *wholesome* reasonable,
salutory.   57 *brace* pair.   60 *desert* merits.   62 *not mine* F³; F¹: "but mine."

3. CIT.   You must think, if we give you anything, we hope to
gain by you.

COR.   Well then, I pray, your price o' th' consulship?

1. CIT.   The price is, to ask it kindly.

COR.   Kindly, sir, I pray let me ha't. I have wounds to show   70
you, which shall be yours in private. Your good voice,
sir. What say you?

2. CIT.   You shall ha't, worthy sir.

COR.   A match, sir. There's in all two worthy voices begg'd.
I have your alms. Adieu.   75

3. CIT.   But this is something odd.

2. CIT.   An 'twere to give again — but 'tis no matter.

Exeunt [the three Citizens].

Enter two other Citizens.

COR.   Pray you now, if it may stand with the tune of your
voices that I may be consul, I have here the customary
gown.   80

1. CIT.   You have deserved nobly of your country, and you have
not deserved nobly.

COR.   Your enigma?

1. CIT.   You have been a scourge to her enemies; you have been
a rod to her friends. You have not indeed loved the   85
common people.

COR.   You should account me the more virtuous that I have
not been common in my love. I will, sir, flatter my sworn
brother, the people, to earn a dearer estimation of them.

---

69 *kindly* (a) politely (b) naturally, as a member of humankind.   71 *be yours* be
shown to you.   74 *match* bargain.   78 *stand* accord.   84-5 *You have . . . friends*
while you have beaten her enemies with a whip (scourge), you have also beaten
her friends with a rod.   88 *common* indiscriminate.   89 *dearer . . . them*
higher place in their esteem.   90 *condition* trait, quality (that of the flatterer).
gentle the sign of a gentleman.   91 *my hat* the outward sign of my subservience
(when doffed).   92 *insinuating* flattering. *be off* doff my hat.   93-4 *counterfeit
the bewitchment* pretend to have the persuasive powers (witchery).   94 *popular
man* man who courts the people.   95 *bountiful* with bounty, liberally.   100 *seal*

'Tis a condition they account gentle; and since the wis-   90
dom of their choice is rather to have my hat than my
heart, I will practise the insinuating nod and be off to
them most counterfeitly: that is, sir, I will counterfeit
the bewitchment of some popular man and give it
bountiful to the desirers. Therefore, beseech you I may   95
be consul.

2. CIT.   We hope to find you our friend; and therefore give you
our voices heartily.

1. CIT.   You have received many wounds for your country.

COR.   I will not seal your knowledge with showing them. I will   100
make much of your voices, and so trouble you no farther.

BOTH.   The gods give you joy, sir, heartily!
                                    [*Exeunt* Citizens.]

COR.   Most sweet voices!
Better it is to die, better to starve,
Than crave the hire which first we do deserve.   105
Why in this wolvish toge should I stand here
To beg of Hob and Dick that does appear
Their needless vouches? Custom calls me to't.
What custom wills, in all things should we do't,
The dust on antique time would lie upswept,   110
And mountainous error be too highly heapt
For truth to o'erpeer. Rather than fool it so,
Let the high office and the honour go
To one that would do thus. I am half through;
The one part suffer'd, the other will I do.   115

Enter three Citizens *more.*

Here come moe voices. —

---

your knowledge confirm what you already know.   105 *hire . . . deserve* reward
which we have already earned by merit.   106 *wolvish* falsely worn (like the wolf
in sheep's clothing).   *toge* toga (MALONE; F¹: "tongue").   107 *Hob and Dick*
rustic names for Robert and Richard.   *does* F¹; F⁴, K: "do."   108 *needless vouches*
unnecessary votes of approval (since I am already entitled to the office by my own
merits).   109 *What custom . . . we do't* if we should do what custom demands
in all instances.   112 *o'erpeer* overtop.   *fool it so* act the fool in that way.   115
suffer'd having undergone.   116 *moe* more.

Your voices! For your voices I have fought;
Watch'd for your voices; for your voices bear
Of wounds two dozen odd; battles thrice six
I have seen and heard of; for your voices have   120
Done many things, some less, some more. Your voices!
Indeed I would be consul.

1. CIT.   He has done nobly and cannot go without any honest
man's voice.

2. CIT.   Therefore let him be consul. The gods give him joy and   125
make him good friend to the people!

ALL.   Amen, amen. God save thee, noble Consul!

COR.   Worthy voices!   [Exeunt Citizens.]

                    Enter Menenius, with Brutus and
                    Sicinius.

MEN.   You have stood your limitation, and the tribunes
           Endue you with the people's voice. Remains   130
           That, in th' official marks invested, you
           Anon do meet the Senate.

COR.   Is this done?

SIC.   The custom of request you have discharg'd.
           The people do admit you, and are summon'd
           To meet anon upon your approbation.   135

COR.   Where? at the Senate House?

SIC.   There, Coriolanus.

COR.   May I change these garments?

SIC.   You may, sir.

COR.   That I'll straight do and, knowing myself again,
           Repair to th' Senate House.

MEN.   I'll keep you company. — Will you along?   140

118 *Watch'd* gone without sleep at night.   129 *your limitation* for your ap-
pointed time.   130 *Endue* endow. *Remains* it remains.   131 *in . . . invested*
wearing the official insignia of office.   133 *custom of request* customary form of
requesting (the people's approval).   135 *upon your approbation* for the purpose
of confirming your election.   138 *knowing myself* being what I truly am (rather

BRU.   We stay here for the people.

SIC.   Fare you well.

Exeunt Coriolanus *and* Menenius.

He has it now; and by his looks, methinks,
'Tis warm at's heart.

BRU.   With a proud heart he wore
His humble weeds. Will you dismiss the people?

Enter the Plebeians.

SIC.   How now, my masters? Have you chose this man?   145

1. CIT.   He has our voices, sir.

BRU.   We pray the gods he may deserve your loves.

2. CIT.   Amen, sir. To my poor unworthy notice,
He mock'd us when he begg'd our voices.

3. CIT.   Certainly
He flouted us downright.   150

1. CIT.   No, 'tis his kind of speech; he did not mock us.

2. CIT.   Not one amongst us, save yourself, but says
He us'd us scornfully. He should have show'd us
His marks of merit, wounds receiv'd for's country.

SIC.   Why, so he did, I am sure.

ALL.   No, no! No man saw 'em.   155

3. CIT.   He said he had wounds which he could show in private,
And with his hat, thus waving it in scorn,
"I would be consul," says he. "Aged custom
But by your voices will not so permit me.
Your voices therefore!" When we granted that,   160
Here was "I thank you for your voices, thank you!
Your most sweet voices! Now you have left your voices,
I have no further with you." Was not this mockery?

SIC.   Why either were you ignorant to see't,

than falsely pretending to be a courter of the people).   141 *stay* wait.   143 *'Tis warm at's heart* it pleases him.   144 *weeds* garments.   150 *flouted us downright* mocked us openly.   158 *Aged* long established.   164 *ignorant* too stupid or too unobservant.

165

Or, seeing it, of such childish friendliness
To yield your voices?

BRU.   Could you not have told him
As you were lesson'd? When he had no power
But was a petty servant to the state,
He was your enemy; ever spake against
Your liberties and the charters that you bear   170
I' th' body of the weal; and now, arriving
A place of potency and sway o' th' state,
If he should still malignantly remain
Fast foe to th' plebeii, your voices might
Be curses to yourselves. You should have said   175
That, as his worthy deeds did claim no less
Than what he stood for, so his gracious nature
Would think upon you for your voices and
Translate his malice towards you into love,
Standing your friendly lord.

SIC.   Thus to have said,   180
As you were fore-advis'd, had touch'd his spirit
And tried his inclination; from him pluck'd
Either his gracious promise, which you might,
As cause had call'd you up, have held him to;
Or else it would have gall'd his surly nature,   185
Which easily endures not article
Tying him to aught. So, putting him to rage,
You should have ta'en th' advantage of his choler
And pass'd him unelected.

BRU.   Did you perceive
He did solicit you in free contempt   190

---

167 *lesson'd* instructed.   170 *charters* rights and privileges.   171 *weal* commonwealth.   *arriving* reaching, attaining.   172 *A place . . . state* a position of power
and control in the government.   178 *think . . . voices* remember with kindness
that you gave him your votes.   179 *Translate* transform.   181 *touch'd* tested (as
coins are tested by "touching" with a touchstone).   185 *gall'd* irritated, rubbed
sore.   186 *article* articulation, stipulation, agreement.   188 *choler* anger.   190
free open, undisguised.   194 *heart* courage.   194-5 *Or had . . . judgment* or did
you have tongues which spoke in opposition to the rule of judgment and common sense? To "cry against" is not only to "speak" but also to "rebel against."

When he did need your loves, and do you think
That his contempt shall not be bruising to you
When he hath power to crush? Why, had your bodies
No heart among you? Or had you tongues to cry
Against the rectorship of judgment?

SIC.   Have you,   195
Ere now, denied the asker, and now again,
Of him that did not ask but mock, bestow
Your su'd-for tongues?

3. CIT.   He's not confirm'd; we may deny him yet.

2. CIT.   And will deny him.   200
I'll have five hundred voices of that sound.

1. CIT.   I twice five hundred, and their friends to piece 'em.

BRU.   Get you hence instantly, and tell those friends
They have chose a consul that will from them take
Their liberties; make them of no more voice   205
Than dogs, that are as often beat for barking
As therefore kept to do so.

SIC.   Let them assemble;
And, on a safer judgment, all revoke
Your ignorant election. Enforce his pride
And his old hate unto you. Besides, forget not   210
With what contempt he wore the humble weed;
How in his suit he scorn'd you; but your loves,
Thinking upon his services, took from you
The apprehension of his present portance,
Which most gibingly, ungravely, he did fashion   215

195-8 *Have you . . . tongues* have you not in the past denied your votes to those
who earnestly asked for them, and have you now granted your requested votes
(su'd-for-tongues) to one who did not really ask, but mocked you instead?   199
confirm'd formally installed in office.   202 *piece 'em* add to them.   207 *therefore* for that purpose — to bark.   209 *Enforce* emphasize.   211 *humble weed*
garment of humility.   213-14 *took from . . . portance* prevented you from observing his behaviour in that instance.   215 *gibingly* with taunting and mockery.   *ungravely* without proper seriousness and respect.   *fashion* shape.

After the inveterate hate he bears you.

BRU.   Lay
A fault on us, your tribunes, that we labour'd,
No impediment between, but that you must
Cast your election on him.

SIC.   Say you chose him
More after our commandment than as guided   220
By your own true affections; and that your minds,
Preoccupied with what you rather must do
Than what you should, made you against the grain
To voice him consul. Lay the fault on us.

BRU.   Ay, spare us not. Say we read lectures to you,   225
How youngly he began to serve his country,
How long continued; and what stock he springs of,
The noble house o' th' Marcians; from whence came
That Ancus Marcius, Numa's daughter's son,
Who after great Hostilius here was King;   230
Of the same house Publius and Quintus were,
That our best water brought by conduits hither;
And [Censorinus, who was] nobly nam'd so,
Twice being [by the people chosen] Censor,
Was his great ancestor.

SIC.   One thus descended,   235
That hath beside well in his person wrought
To be set high in place, we did commend
To your remembrances; but you have found,
Scaling his present bearing with his past,
That he's your fixed enemy, and revoke   240
Your sudden approbation.

---

216 *After* in accordance with.   216–17 *Lay . . . us* place the blame on us.   218
No impediment between so that there would be nothing to impede.   220 *after our*
commandment according to our instructions.   221 *affections* feelings, desires.
223 *against the grain* contrary to your natural inclinations.   225 *read lectures*
gave special instructions.   226 *youngly* as a youth.   228 *house o' th' Marcians*
In following Plutarch's list of noble members of this Roman family, Shakespeare
actually includes some members who lived after the time of Coriolanus.   233–4
And [Censorinus] . . . Censor K; F¹: "And Nobly nam'd, so twice being Censor."

BRU.   Say you ne'er had done't
(Harp on that still) but by our putting on;
And presently, when you have drawn your number,
Repair to th' Capitol.

ALL.   We will so. Almost all
Repent in their election.   *Exeunt* Plebeians.

BRU.   Let them go on.   245
This mutiny were better put in hazard
Than stay, past doubt, for greater.
If, as his nature is, he fall in rage
With their refusal, both observe and answer
The vantage of his anger.

SIC.   To th' Capitol, come.   250
We will be there before the stream o' th' people;
And this shall seem, as partly 'tis, their own,
Which we have goaded onward.   *Exeunt.*

The passage in F¹ is obviously corrupt. κ's attempt to supply the missing words
is based closely upon the corresponding passage in Plutarch.   239 *Scaling* weigh-
ing.   241 *sudden approbation* hasty approval.   242 *still* continually. *putting on*
urging.   243 *drawn your number* gathered together a sufficient number of supporters.   246 *mutiny* popular uprising. *put in hazard* risked.   247 *Than . . .
greater* than wait for a greater civil disorder which, without doubt, will come.
249–50 *answer . . . anger* respond to the advantage which his anger will give us.

Act Three

◇◇◇◇◇◇◇◇◇◇◇◇◇◇◇◇◇◇◇◇◇◇◇◇◇◇◇◇◇◇◇◇◇◇◇◇◇◇

[SCENE I. *Rome. A street.*]

Cornets. Enter Coriolanus, Menenius, *all the* Gentry, Cominius, Titus Lartius, *and other* Senators.

COR. Tullus Aufidius, then, had made new head?

LART. He had, my lord, and that it was which caus'd
Our swifter composition.

COR. So then the Volsces stand but as at first,
Ready, when time shall prompt them, to make road   5
Upon's again.

COM.   They are worn, Lord Consul, so
That we shall hardly in our ages see
Their banners wave again.

COR.   Saw you Aufidius?

LART. On safeguard he came to me, and did curse
Against the Volsces for they had so vilely   10
Yielded the town. He is retir'd to Antium.

COR. Spoke he of me?

LART.   He did, my lord.

COR.   How? what?

III.I. 1 *made new head* gathered a new army.   3 *Our swifter composition* our coming to terms with greater speed.   5 *road* inroads, raids.   7 *ages* lifetimes. 9 *On safeguard* under safe-conduct.   10 *for* because.   11 *is retir'd* has retreated. 16 *To hopeless restitution* beyond all hope of recovery.   23 *prank them* dress

LART.   How often he had met you sword to sword;
        That of all things upon the earth he hated
        Your person most; that he would pawn his fortunes   15
        To hopeless restitution, so he might
        Be call'd your vanquisher.

COR.   At Antium lives he?

LART.   At Antium.

COR.   I wish I had a cause to seek him there,
        To oppose his hatred fully. Welcome home.   20

                    Enter Sicinius *and* Brutus.

        Behold, these are the tribunes of the people,
        The tongues o' th' common mouth. I do despise them,
        For they do prank them in authority
        Against all noble sufferance.

SIC.   Pass no further.

COR.   Ha! What is that?   25

BRU.   It will be dangerous to go on. No further.

COR.   What makes this change?

MEN.   The matter?

COM.   Hath he not pass'd the noble and the common?

BRU.   Cominius, no.

COR.   Have I had children's voices?   30

1. SEN. Tribune's, give way. He shall to th' market place.

BRU.   The people are incens'd against him.

SIC.   Stop,
        Or all will fall in broil.

COR.   Are these your herd?

---

themselves up.   24 *Against . . . sufferance* in a way that no nobleman can endure.   29 *pass'd . . . common* been approved by both the nobles and the commons.   30 *children's voices* votes which may be given and then taken back.   33
broil tumult, uproar.

Must these have voices, that can yield them now
And straight disclaim their tongues? What are your offices? 35
You being their mouths, why rule you not their teeth?
Have you not set them on?

MEN.   Be calm, be calm.

COR.   It is a purpos'd thing and grows by plot
To curb the will of the nobility.
Suffer't, and live with such as cannot rule   40
Nor ever will be rul'd.

BRU.   Call't not a plot.
The people cry you mock'd them; and of late,
When corn was given them gratis, you repin'd;
Scandal'd the suppliants for the people, call'd them
Time-pleasers, flatterers, foes to nobleness.   45

COR.   Why, this was known before.

BRU.   Not to them all.

COR.   Have you inform'd them sithence?

BRU.   How? I inform them?

COR.   You are like to do such business.

BRU.   Not unlike
Each way to better yours.

COR.   Why then should I be consul? By yond clouds,   50
Let me deserve so ill as you, and make me
Your fellow tribune.

SIC.   You show too much of that
For which the people stir. If you will pass
To where you are bound, you must inquire your way,

---

35 *disclaim their tongues* deny the validity of their own votes.   36 *rule . . . teeth*
prevent them from biting. The common people are compared to a herd of wild
animals.   37 *set them on* incited them.   38 *purpos'd thing* contrived affair.   40
Suffer't permit it.   43 *repin'd* expressed regret.   44 *Scandal'd* insulted.   47
sithence since.   48 *You . . . business* THEOBALD; F¹ gives the speech to Cominius
and may well be correct.   48–9 *Not unlike . . . yours* likely in every way to do
better than you would do (if you were consul).   50 *By yond clouds* a mild oath.
52 *show* reveal.   *that* i.e. tyranny.   53 *For . . . stir* because of which the people
rise up.   53–4 *pass . . . bound* move to your objective — the consulship.   57
yoke with him for be joined with him as.   58 *abus'd* deceived.   *set on* incited.

	Which you are out of, with a gentler spirit,	55
	Or never be so noble as a consul	
	Nor yoke with him for tribune.	

MEN.   Let's be calm.

COM.   The people are abus'd, set on. This palt'ring
        Becomes not Rome; nor has Coriolanus
        Deserv'd this so dishonour'd rub, laid falsely   60
        I' th' plain way of his merit.

COR.   Tell me of corn!
        This was my speech, and I will speak't again —

MEN.   Not now! not now!

1. SEN.   Not in this heat, sir, now.

COR.   Now, as I live, I will! My nobler friends,
        I crave their pardons.   65
        For the mutable, rank-scented meiny, let them
        Regard me as I do not flatter, and
        Therein behold themselves. I say again,
        In soothing them we nourish 'gainst our Senate
        The cockle of rebellion, insolence, sedition,   70
        Which we ourselves have ploug'd for, sow'd, and scatter'd
        By mingling them with us, the honour'd number,
        Who lack not virtue, no, nor power, but that
        Which they have given to beggars.

MEN.   Well, no more.

1. SEN. No more words, we beseech you.

COR.   How? No more?   75
        As for my country I have shed my blood,
        Not fearing outward force, so shall my lungs

---

palt'ring trickery, equivocation.   60 *dishonour'd* dishonourable.   *rub* impediment, obstacle (a term from the game of bowls, referring to any obstruction which
impedes the path of the bowl on its proper course).   63 *heat* anger.   66 *mutable*
ever-changing, fickle.   *rank-scented* evil-smelling.   *meiny* crowd, rabble.   67 *as
I do not flatter* as I speak of them when not flattering (as opposed to my former
speech when wearing the gown of humility).   70 *cockle* a weed common to wheat-
fields.   73-4 *Who lack . . . beggars* who (the aristocrats) still have ample virtue
and power, lacking only what has been granted to the common people (beggars)
by them.

Coin words till their decay against those measles
Which we disdain should tetter us, yet sought
The very way to catch them.

BRU.   You speak o' th' people   80
As if you were a god to punish, not
A man of their infirmity.

SIC.   'Twere well
We let the people know't.

MEN.   What, what? his choler?

COR.   Choler?
Were I as patient as the midnight sleep,   85
By Jove, 'twould be my mind!

SIC.   It is a mind
That shall remain a poison where it is,
Not poison any further.

COR.   Shall remain?
Hear you this Triton of the minnows? Mark you
His absolute "shall"?

COM.   'Twas from the canon.

COR.   "Shall"?   90
O good but most unwise patricians! Why,
You grave but reckless senators, have you thus
Given Hydra here to choose an officer
That was his peremptory "shall," being but
The horn and noise o' th' monster's, wants not spirit   95
To say he'll turn your current in a ditch
And make your channel his? If he have power,

---

78 *decay* death.   *measles* The term was applied both to leprosy and to sores caused
by the plague.   79 *tetter us* cover our bodies with the "tetter," a general term
for any skin eruption.   82 *infirmity* ordinary human weakness.   89 *Triton* a
sea deity, the trumpeter of Neptune, whose duty it is to calm the waves.   90
from the canon contrary to the rule of law. The tribune's function is merely to
speak for the people, not to establish the law.   91 *O good* THEOBALD; F¹: "O God!"
93 *Hydra* the many-headed monster of Greek mythology — i.e. the people.   95
horn and noise noisy horn. Triton carried a horn; he is here identified as the
voice of the Hydra, both classical references being fused.   96–7 *turn your . . .
channel his* divert your (the Patricians') water supply into a ditch and take

Then vail your ignorance; if none, awake
Your dangerous lenity. If you are learn'd,
Be not as common fools; if you are not,   100
Let them have cushions by you. You are plebeians
If they be senators; and they are no less
When, both your voices blended, the great'st taste
Most palates theirs. They choose their magistrate;
And such a one as he, who puts his "shall,"   105
His popular "shall," against a graver bench
Than ever frown'd in Greece. By Jove himself,
It makes the consuls base! and my soul aches
To know, when two authorities are up,
Neither supreme, how soon confusion   110
May enter 'twixt the gap of both and take
The one by th' other.

COM.   Well, on to th' market place.

COR.   Whoever gave that counsel to give forth
The corn o' th' storehouse gratis, as 'twas us'd
Sometime in Greece —

MEN.   Well, well, no more of that.   115

COR.   Though there the people had more absolute pow'r —
I say they nourish'd disobedience, fed
The ruin of the state.

BRU.   Why, shall the people give
One that speaks thus their voice?

COR.   I'll give my reasons,
More worthier than their voices. They know the corn   120

---

possession of your conduit for his own use.   97–8 *If he . . . ignorance* if he (the Tribune) have power, let you, who ignorantly gave it to him, bow down before him.   98–9 *if none . . . lenity* if he have no power, arouse your dangerous mildness (into action).   101 *cushions* seats upon which senators sat. *by you* along side of you (in the Senate).   102–4 *and they . . . palates theirs* and they are no less than senators when, sitting together and combining your voices in a common decision, the common decision tastes of their opinion, i.e. if they have any role at all in government.   106 *popular* vulgar.   109 *are up* are in action.   111–12 *enter 'twixt . . . th' other* come between the two and destroy both, the one by means of the other.   114 *us'd* practiced.   115 *Sometime* once.

Was not our recompense, resting well assur'd
They ne'er did service for't. Being press'd to th' war
Even when the navel of the state was touch'd,
They would not thread the gates. This kind of service
Did not deserve corn gratis. Being i' th' war,   125
Their mutinies and revolts, wherein they show'd
Most valour, spoke not for them. Th' accusation
Which they have often made against the Senate,
All cause unborn, could never be the motive
Of our so frank donation. Well, what then?   130
How shall this bosom multiplied digest
The Senate's courtesy? Let deeds express
What's like to be their words: "We did request it;
We are the greater poll, and in true fear
They gave us our demands." Thus we debase   135
The nature of our seats and make the rabble
Call our cares fears; which will in time break ope
The locks o' th' Senate and bring in the crows
To peck the eagles.

MEN.   Come, enough.

BRU.   Enough, with over-measure.

COR.   No, take more!   140
What may be sworn by, both divine and human,
Seal what I end withal! This double worship —
Where one part does disdain with cause, the other
Insult without all reason; where gentry, title, wisdom
Cannot conclude but by the yea and no   145
Of general ignorance — it must omit

---

121 *our recompense* intended by us as a reward for their services.   122 *press'd*
drafted.   123 *navel* vital centre.   *touch'd* threatened.   124 *thread* pass through.
129 *All cause unborn* without justification.   *motive* JOHNSON; F¹: "native," which
many editors retain as meaning "origin."   130 *frank* freely given.   131 *bosom
multiplied* heart of the common people — a single bosom multiplied many times
(F¹; K: "beesom multitude").   *digest* interpret, understand.   132-3 *Let deeds
. . . their words* let their deeds give us an indication of what they are likely to
say.   134 *greater poll* majority.   137 *cares* concerns (for their welfare).   140
over-measure excess.   142 *Seal* confirm.   *withal* with.   *double worship* two centres
of authority.   144 *without* beyond.   *gentry, title, wisdom* gentlemen, nobility,
wise men.   145 *conclude* make decisions.   146 *general ignorance* the ignorant
populace.   *omit* neglect.   148 *unstable slightness* inconsequential and frivolous

Real necessities, and give way the while
To unstable slightness. Purpose so barr'd, it follows
Nothing is done to purpose. Therefore, beseech you —
You that will be less fearful than discreet;   150
That love the fundamental part of state
More than you doubt the change on't; that prefer
A noble life before a long, and wish
To jump a body with a dangerous physic
That's sure of death without it — at once pluck out   155
The multitudinous tongue; let them not lick
The sweet which is their poison. Your dishonour
Mangles true judgment, and bereaves the state
Of that integrity which should become't,
Not having the power to do the good it would   160
For th' ill which doth control't.

BRU.   Has said enough.

SIC.   Has spoken like a traitor and shall answer
As traitors do.

COR.   Thou wretch, despite o'erwhelm thee!
What should the people do with these bald tribunes?   165
On whom depending, their obedience fails
To th' greater bench. In a rebellion,
When what's not meet, but what must be, was law,
Then were they chosen. In a better hour,
Let what is meet be said it must be meet,   170
And throw their power i' th' dust.

BRU.   Manifest treason!

---

trifles. *Purpose so barr'd* serious business so thwarted.   149 *to purpose* of real
consequence.   150 *discreet* prudent.   151 *fundamental part of state* essential
character of our government.   152 *doubt the change on't* fear the turmoil which
springs from attempts to change it, i.e. revolution.   154–5 *jump . . . without it*
risk a dangerous cure upon a body certain of death if left uncured.   156 *multitudinous tongue* those who speak for the multitude — the Tribunes.   156 *them*
the people.   157 *sweet* flattery.   159 *integrity* singleness of purpose.   161 *For*
because of.   *Has* he has.   162 *answer* suffer the consequences.   164 *despite* contempt.   165 *bald* paltry.   167 *th' greater bench* the Senate.   168 *meet* fitting,
proper.   170 *Let what . . . be meet* let it be said (to the people) that what is
actually fitting must be regarded as fitting (carried out).

SIC.   This a consul? No.

BRU.   The ædiles, ho!

                    Enter an Ædile.

                    Let him be apprehended.

SIC.   Go call the people, [*exit Ædile*] in whose name myself
         Attach thee as a traitorous innovator,   175
         A foe to th' public weal. Obey, I charge thee,
         And follow to thine answer.

COR.   Hence, old goat!

ALL [PATRICIANS]. We'll surety him.

COM.   Aged sir, hands off.

COR.   Hence, rotten thing! or I shall shake thy bones
         Out of thy garments.

SIC.   Help, ye citizens!   180

                    Enter a rabble of Plebeians, *with the*
                    Ædiles.

MEN.   On both sides more respect.

SIC.   Here's he that would take from you all your power.

BRU.   Seize him, ædiles!

ALL [PLEBEIANS]. Down with him! down with him!

2. SEN. Weapons, weapons, weapons!   185

                    They all bustle about Coriolanus,
                    [*crying*]:

         Tribunes! — Patricians! — Citizens! — What, ho! —
         Sicinius! — Brutus! — Coriolanus! — Citizens!

ALL [PATRICIANS]. Peace, peace, peace! Stay, hold, peace!

MEN.   What is about to be? I am out of breath.

---

173 *ædiles* magistrates who served as assistants to the Tribunes.   175 *Attach* arrest. *innovator* revolutionary.   177 *answer* trial.   178 *surety* provide bail for.
190 *Confusion* ruin.   194 *at point to* about to.   206 *distinctly ranges* extends
out (like rows of houses) in an orderly fashion.   208 *Or let us stand to* either let

Confusion's near. I cannot speak. You, Tribunes, 190
Speak to th' people. Coriolanus, patience.
Speak, good Sicinius.

SIC. Hear me, people. Peace!

ALL [PLEBEIANS]. Let's hear our tribune. Peace! Speak, speak,
speak!

SIC. You are at point to lose your liberties.
Marcius would have all from you, Marcius, 195
Whom late you have nam'd for consul.

MEN. Fie, fie, fie!
This is the way to kindle, not to quench.

1. SEN. To unbuild the city and to lay all flat.

SIC. What is the city but the people?

ALL [PLEBEIANS]. True!
The people are the city. 200

BRU. By the consent of all we were establish'd
The people's magistrates.

ALL [PLEBEIANS]. You so remain.

MEN. And so are like to do.

COM. That is the way to lay the city flat,
To bring the roof to the foundation. 205
And bury all which yet distinctly ranges
In heaps and piles of ruin.

SIC. This deserves death.

BRU. Or let us stand to our authority
Or let us lose it. We do here pronounce
Upon the part o' th' people, in whose power 210
We were elected theirs, Marcius is worthy
Of present death.

SIC. Therefore lay hold of him.
Bear him to th' Rock Tarpeian and from thence

us insist upon. 210 *Upon the part* in the name. 212 *present* immediate. 213
Rock Tarpeian a steep rock on the Capitoline Hill from which traitors were
thrown to their deaths below.

Into destruction cast him.

BRU.   Ædiles, seize him!

ALL PLEBEIANS. Yield, Marcius, yield!

MEN.   Hear me one word.   215
Beseech you, Tribunes, hear me but a word.

ÆDILES. Peace, peace!

MEN.   [*to* Brutus] Be that you seem, truly your country's
         friend
And temp'rately proceed to what you would
Thus violently redress.

BRU.   Sir, those cold ways   220
That seem like prudent helps are very poisonous
Where the disease is violent. — Lay hands upon him
And bear him to the Rock.

Coriolanus draws his sword.

COR.   No, I'll die here.
There's some among you have beheld me fighting.
Come try upon yourselves what you have seen me.   225

MEN.   Down with that sword! Tribunes, withdraw awhile.

BRU.   Lay hands upon him.

MEN.   Help Marcius, help!
You that be noble, help him, young and old!

ALL [PLEBEIANS]. Down with him! down with him!

In this mutiny the Tribunes, *the*
Ædiles, *and the* People *are beat in.*

MEN.   Go, get you to your house! Be gone, away!   230

---

218 *that you seem* that which you pretend to be.   219–20 *temp'rately . . . redress*
calmly and carefully work toward the objective you are now trying to achieve
by violence.   220 *cold* calm, passionless.   225 *seen me* seen me perform.   230
to your ROWE; F¹: "to our."   231 *naught else* ruined otherwise.   231–2 *Stand
. . . enemies* WARBURTON; F¹ gives the speech to Cominius and may well be correct.
235 *cause* disease. *For* because.   236 *You cannot tent* which you cannot cure.
A "tent" was a gauze dressing placed in a wound in order to cleanse it.   237
Come . . . us F²; F¹ gives the speech to Coriolanus.   238–40 *I would . . . Cap-*

All will be naught else.

2. SEN.   Get you gone.

COR.   Stand fast!
We have as many friends as enemies.

MEN.   Shall it be put to that?

1. SEN.   The gods forbid!
I prithee, noble friend, home to thy house.
Leave us to cure this cause.

MEN.   For 'tis a sore upon us   235
You cannot tent yourself. Be gone, beseech you.

COM.   Come, sir, along with us.

COR.   I would they were barbarians, as they are,
Though in Rome litter'd; not Romans, as they are not,
Though calv'd i' th' porch o' th' Capitol.

MEN.   Be gone.   240
Put not your worthy rage into your tongue.
One time will owe another.

COR.   On fair ground
I could beat forty of them.

MEN.   I could myself
Take up a brace o' th' best of them; yea, the two trib-
    unes.

COM.   But now 'tis odds beyond arithmetic,   245
And manhood is call'd foolery when it stands
Against a falling fabric. Will you hence
Before the tag return? whose rage doth rend
Like interrupted waters, and o'erbear

---

itol TYRWHITT; F¹ gives these lines to Menenius as part of his following speech.
litter'd . . . calv'd He contemptuously refers to the birth of these Romans as
though they were swine or cattle.   241 *worthy rage* anger which is justified and
thus does you credit.   242 *One time . . . another* another time will make up for
this one.   244 *Take up* defeat in a fight. *brace* pair.   245 *beyond arithmetic*
too great to be calculated.   247 *fabric* building.   248 *tag* rabble. *rend* tear down
(all before them).   249 *interrupted waters* flood waters — rivers that have burst
their banks. *o'erbear* overpower.

What they are us'd to bear.

MEN.   Pray you be gone.   250
I'll try whether my old wit be in request
With those that have but little. This must be patch'd
With cloth of any colour.

COM.   Nay, come away.

> *Exeunt* Coriolanus *and* Cominius,
> [*with others*].

PATRICIAN. This man has marr'd his fortune.

MEN.   His nature is too noble for the world.   255
He would not flatter Neptune for his trident
Or Jove for's power to thunder. His heart's his mouth;
What his breast forges, that his tongue must vent,
And being angry does forget that ever
He heard the name of death.   *A noise within.* 260
Here's goodly work!

PATRICIAN.   I would they were abed!

MEN.   I would they were in Tiber! What the vengeance,
Could he not speak 'em fair?

> *Enter* Brutus *and* Sicinius *with the*
> Rabble *again*.

SIC.   Where is this viper
That would depopulate the city and
Be every man himself?

MEN.   You worthy Tribunes —   265

SIC.   He shall be thrown down the Tarpeian Rock
With rigorous hands. He hath resisted law,
And therefore law shall scorn him further trial
Than the severity of the public power,
Which he so sets at naught.

---

250 *us'd to bear* accustomed to endure (as restraining forces).   256 *trident* three-
pronged fork.   258 *vent* express.   263 *speak 'em fair* speak courteously to them.
268 *scorn him* scornfully deny him.   274 *cry havoc* give the signal for indiscriminate slaughter with no taking of prisoners.   275 *With modest warrant as* mod-

1. CIT.   He shall well know   270
   The noble tribunes are the people's mouths,
   And we their hands.

ALL [PLEBEIANS].
              He shall, sure on't!

MEN.   Sir, sir —

SIC.   Peace!

MEN.   Do not cry havoc where you should but hunt
   With modest warrant.

SIC.   Sir, how comes't that you   275
   Have holp to make this rescue?

MEN.   Hear me speak.
   As I do know the consul's worthiness,
   So can I name his faults.

SIC.   Consul? What consul?

MEN.   The consul Coriolanus.

BRU.   He consul?

ALL [PLEBEIANS]. No, no, no, no, no!   280

MEN.   If, by the tribunes' leave, and yours, good people,
   I may be heard, I would crave a word or two,
   The which shall turn you to no further harm
   Than so much loss of time.

SIC.   Speak briefly then,
   For we are peremptory to dispatch   285
   This viperous traitor. To eject him hence
   Were but our danger, and to keep him here
   Our certain death. Therefore it is decreed
   He dies to-night.

MEN.   Now the good gods forbid
   That our renowned Rome, whose gratitude   290

---

eration would prescribe.   276 *holp* helped.   *rescue* prevention of arrest (of
Coriolanus).   283 *turn you to* cause you.   285 *peremptory* firmly resolved.   *dispatch* execute.   286-7 *To eject . . . danger* to exile him would be to subject
ourselves to danger.   *our danger* THEOBALD; F¹: "one danger."

Towards her deserved children is enroll'd
In Jove's own book, like an unnatural dam
Should now eat up her own!

SIC. He's a disease that must be cut away.

MEN. O, he's a limb that has but a disease: 295
Mortal, to cut it off; to cure it, easy.
What has he done to Rome that's worthy death?
Killing our enemies, the blood he hath lost
(Which, I dare vouch, is more than that he hath,
By many an ounce) he dropp'd it for his country;   300
And what is left, to lose it by his country
Were to us all that do't and suffer it
A brand to th' end o' th' world.

SIC.   This is clean kam.

BRU. Merely awry. When he did love his country,
It honour'd him.

MEN.   The service of the foot,   305
Being once gangren'd, is not then respected
For what before it was.

BRU.   We'll hear no more.
Pursue him to his house and pluck him thence,
Lest his infection, being of catching nature,
Spread further.

MEN.   One word more, one word!   310
This tiger-footed rage, when it shall find
The harm of unscann'd swiftness, will (too late)
Tie leaden pounds to's heels. Proceed by process,
Lest parties (as he is belov'd) break out
And sack great Rome with Romans.

291 *deserved* meritorious, deserving of honour.   291–2 *enroll'd . . . book* inscribed as law in the book of laws in the Capitol, which was the temple of Jove. 292 *dam* mother.   297 *worthy* deserving of.   303 *brand* mark of infamy. Criminals were branded with hot irons for certain offences.   *clean* entirely.   *kam* perverse, contrary (a Celtic word meaning literally "crooked" or "bent").   304 *Merely awry* entirely twisted.   305–7 *The service . . . it was* Nineteenth century editors often assigned this speech to Brutus or Sicinius as being more appropriate to one of them, but there is no need to depart from the F[1] text. Menenius is echoing the sentiments of the tribunes with bitter irony.   312 *unscann'd swiftness*

BRU.   If it were so —   315

SIC.   What do ye talk?
       Have we not had a taste of his obedience —
       Our ædiles smote? ourselves resisted? Come!

MEN.   Consider this: he has been bred i' th' wars
       Since 'a could draw a sword, and is ill-school'd   320
       In bolted language; meal and bran together
       He throws without distinction. Give me leave,
       I'll go to him and undertake to bring him
       Where he shall answer by a lawful form
       (In peace) to his utmost peril.

1. SEN.   Noble Tribunes,   325
       It is the humane way. The other course
       Will prove too bloody, and the end of it
       Unknown to the beginning.

SIC.   Noble Menenius,
       Be you then as the people's officer.
       Masters, lay down your weapons.

BRU.   Go not home.   330

SIC.   Meet on the market place. We'll attend you there,
       Where if you bring not Marcius, we'll proceed
       In our first way.

MEN.   I'll bring him to you.
       [*To the* Senators] Let me desire your company. He must
           come,
       Or what is worst will follow.

1. SEN.   Pray you, let's to him.   335
                                    Exeunt omnes.

---

haste without due consideration.   313 *pounds* weights.   *to's* to its (swiftness's).
process legal procedure.   314 *parties* factions.   315 *sack . . . Romans* destroy
Rome by the actions of Romans themselves.   317 *taste* example.   318 *smote*
smitten.   321 *bolted language* refined, elegant speech. To "bolt" is to "sift" as
flour is sifted.   323 *bring him* POPE; F[1]: "bring him in peace."   324-5 *answer
. . . peril* defend himself against the charges against him in a proper legal trial,
no matter how severe the judgment against him is likely to be.   327-8 *the end
. . . beginning* the results of such action incapable of being foreseen at the time
the action is undertaken.   331 *attend* wait for.   334 *Desire* request.

◇◇◇◇◇◇◇◇◇◇◇◇◇◇◇◇◇

[SCENE II.
A room in the house of Coriolanus.]

Enter Coriolanus *with* Nobles.

COR.   Let them pull all about mine ears; present me
Death on the wheel or at wild horses' heels;
Or pile ten hills on the Tarpeian Rock,
That the precipitation might down stretch
Below the beam of sight — yet will I still   5
Be thus to them.

NOBLE.   You do the nobler.

COR.   I muse my mother
Does not approve me further, who was wont
To call them woollen vassals, things created
To buy and sell with groats, to show bare heads   10
In congregations, to yawn, be still, and wonder
When one but of my ordinance stood up
To speak of peace or war.

Enter Volumnia.

                    I talk of you.
Why did you wish me milder? Would you have me
False to my nature? Rather say, I play   15
The man I am.

VOL.   O, sir, sir, sir!
I would have had you put your power well on
Before you had worn it out.

III.II. 2 *the wheel* an instrument of torture used in Renaissance Europe but
unknown in classical times. *at wild horses' heels* Tearing to pieces by wild horses
was another punishment unknown to the Romans. 4 *precipitation* precipice. 5
beam range. 7 *muse* am astonished that. 8 *approve me further* show more
approval of my conduct. *wont* accustomed. 9 *woolen vassals* slaves dressed in
coarse clothing. 10 *groats* fourpenny pieces in Elizabethan London. Thus the
trading referred to is of a very petty kind. 11 *congregations* assemblies. 12

COR.	Let go.

VOL. You might have been enough the man you are
   With striving less to be so. Lesser had been   20
   The thwarting of your dispositions, if
   You had not show'd them how ye were dispos'd
   Ere they lack'd power to cross you.

COR.   Let them hang.

VOL. Ay, and burn too!

      Enter Menenius *with the* Senators.

MEN. Come, come, you have been too rough, something too
    rough.   25
   You must return and mend it.

SENATOR.   There's no remedy,
   Unless, by not so doing, our good city
   Cleave in the midst and perish.

VOL.   Pray be counsell'd.
   I have a heart as little apt as yours,
   But yet a brain that leads my use of anger   30
   To better vantage.

MEN.   Well said, noble woman!
   Before he should thus stoop to th' herd, but that
   The violent fit o' th' time craves it as physic
   For the whole state, I would put mine armour on,
   Which I can scarcely bear.

COR.   What must I do?   35

MEN. Return to th' tribunes.

COR.   Well, what then? what then?

MEN. Repent what you have spoke.

---

ordinance social rank. 17–18 *put your . . . it out* The metaphor treats power
as a suit of clothes. 18 *Let go* enough; desist (F¹; K: "Let't go"). 21 *thwarting*
K; THEOBALD: "thwartings"; F¹: "things." *dispositions* inclinations. 23 *cross* op-
pose. 25 *something* somewhat. 26 *mend it* amend your behaviour. 28 *Cleave
in the midst* be divided in the centre. 29 *as little apt* as stubborn. 31 *vantage*
advantage. 32 *th' herd* THEOBALD; F¹: "th' heart." 33 *fit* disease. *craves* requires.
physic medicine.

COR.   For them? I cannot do it to the gods.
         Must I then do't to them?

VOL.   You are too absolute;
         Though therein you can never be too noble,   40
         But when extremities speak. I have heard you say,
         Honour and policy, like unsever'd friends,
         I' th' war do grow together. Grant that, and tell me,
         In peace what each of them by th' other lose,
         That they combine not there.

COR.   Tush, tush!

MEN.   A good demand.   45

VOL.   If it be honour in your wars to seem
         The same you are not, — which, for your best ends,
         You adopt your policy, — how is it less or worse
         That it shall hold companionship in peace
         With honour, as in war; since that to both   50
         It stands in like request?

COR.   Why force you this?

VOL.   Because that now it lies you on to speak
         To th' people, not by your own instruction,
         Nor by th' matter which your heart prompts you,
         But with such words that are but roted in   55
         Your tongue, though but bastards and syllables
         Of no allowance to your bosom's truth.
         Now, this no more dishonours you at all
         Than to take in a town with gentle words

---

39 *absolute* inflexible.   41 *extremities speak* special crises demand (special action).
42 *policy* strategy, prudent behaviour (but the word had come to mean "political
trickery").   *unsever'd* inseparable.   44–5 *In peace . . . not there* what each would
lose in peacetime if not combined with the other (as they are combined in war).
45 *demand* question to be considered.   46–7 *seem . . . not* pretend to be what
you really are not.   49 *it* policy.   50–1 *since that . . . request* since it (policy)
is required equally in both instances (peace and war). Why is it less honourable,
she is asking, to practise policy in time of peace than in time of war.   51 *force*
urge.   52 *lies you on* is incumbent upon you.   55 *roted* merely learned by rote
(F¹: "roated"; some editors read "rooted").   56–7 *bastards . . . bosom's truth*
The words, being insincere, are conceived of as illegitimate offspring of his heart,
having no real relation to his true feelings.   59 *take in* capture.   60 *else . . .
fortune* otherwise cause you to run a risk (of loss in battle).   62 *dissemble with*

Which else would put you to your fortune and 60
The hazard of much blood.
I would dissemble with my nature where
My fortunes and my friends at stake requir'd
I should do so in honour. I am in this
Your wife, your son, these senators, the nobles; 65
And you will rather show our general louts
How you can frown than spend a fawn upon 'em
For the inheritance of their loves and safeguard
Of what that want might ruin.

MEN.   Noble lady!
Come, go with us. Speak fair. You may salve so, 70
Not what is dangerous present, but the loss
Of what is past.

VOL.   I prithee now, my son,
Go to them, with this bonnet in thy hand;
And thus far having stretch'd it (here be with them),
Thy knee bussing the stones (for in such business 75
Action is eloquence, and the eyes of th' ignorant
More learned than the ears), waving thy head,
Which often, thus, correcting thy stout heart,
Now humble as the ripest mulberry
That will not hold the handling — say to them 80
Thou art their soldier, and, being bred in broils,
Hast not the soft way which, thou dost confess,
Were fit for thee to use, as they to claim,
In asking their good loves; but thou wilt frame

---

my nature pretend to be something contrary to my true nature — play the hypo-
crite.   63–4 *My fortunes . . . honour* She seems to be suggesting that such dis-
sembling for the sake of country and friends may constitute a higher kind of
honour than mere fidelity to one's own nature.   64 *I am in this* in speaking thus
I represent.   66 *general* vulgar.   67 *fawn* appeal by flattery.   68 *inheritance*
obtaining, acquisition.   69 *want* lack — of their "loves."   70 *salve* remedy.   71
Not . . . present not only the present danger.   71–2 *loss . . . past* that which
you have already lost — the consulship.   73 *bonnet* cap.   74 *And thus* Volumnia
by her actions indicates the gestures Coriolanus is to make.   75 *bussing* kissing.
78 *correcting . . . heart* chastening the natural impulses of your brave heart.   79
mulberry This was a traditional symbol of falseness and treachery because a serpent in medieval iconography usually lurked in the mulberry tree.   80 *hold*
endure.   81 *broils* battles.   84 *frame* make.

Thyself (forsooth) hereafter theirs, so far   85
As thou hast power and person.

MEN.   This but done
Even as she speaks, why, their hearts were yours!
For they have pardons, being ask'd, as free
As words to little purpose.

VOL.   Prithee now,
Go, and be rul'd; although I know thou hadst rather   90
Follow thine enemy in a fiery gulf
Than flatter him in a bower.

Enter Cominius.

                                    Here is Cominius.

COM.   I have been i' th' market place; and, sir, 'tis fit
You make strong party, or defend yourself
By calmness or by absence. All's in anger.   95

MEN.   Only fair speech.

COM.   I think 'twill serve, if he
Can thereto frame his spirit.

VOL.   He must and will.
Prithee now, say you will, and go about it.

COR.   Must I go show them my unbarb'd sconce? Must I
With my base tongue give to my noble heart   100
A lie that it must bear? Well, I will do't.
Yet, were there but this single plot to lose,
This mould of Marcius, they to dust should grind it
And throw't against the wind. To th' market place!

---

85 *theirs* as they would wish.   88–9 *For they . . . purpose* Shakespeare affirms
the native kindness and generosity of the common people at the same time that
he censures their wisdom in political affairs. They will gladly give their pardons
in return for a few trifling words of little real significance.   91 *fiery gulf* flaming
pit.   92 *bower* lady's chamber (associated with love-making).   94 *make strong
party* have a large body of supporters.   99 *unbarb'd* unprotected, unarmed.
sconce head.   102 *plot* body (conceived of as a small portion of earth).   103
mould bodily shape.   105–6 *put me . . . to th' life* assigned me such a role that
I will never be able to perform convincingly. The metaphor is drawn from the
theatre.   111 *possess me* let me be possessed by.   112 *harlot's* false rascal's. The
term was sometimes applied to men as well as women.   113 *quier'd with* sang

You have put me now to such a part which never 105
I shall discharge to th' life.

COM.   Come, come, we'll prompt you.

VOL. I prithee now, sweet son, as thou hast said
My praises made thee first a soldier, so,
To have my praise for this, perform a part
Thou hast not done before.

COR.   Well, I must do't. 110
Away, my disposition, and possess me
Some harlot's spirit! My throat of war be turn'd,
Which quier'd with my drum, into a pipe
Small as an eunuch or the virgin voice
That babies lulls asleep! The smiles of knaves 115
Tent in my cheeks, and schoolboys' tears take up
The glasses of my sight! A beggar's tongue
Make motion through my lips, and my arm'd knees,
Who bow'd but in my stirrup, bend like his
That hath receiv'd an alms! I will not do't, 120
Lest I surcease to honour mine own truth
And by my body's action teach my mind
A most inherent baseness.

VOL.   At thy choice then.
To beg of thee, it is my more dishonour
Than thou of them. Come all to ruin! Let 125
Thy mother rather feel thy pride than fear
Thy dangerous stoutness; for I mock at death
With as big heart as thou. Do as thou list.
Thy valiantness was mine, thou suck'st it from me;

in a chorus with. *pipe* voice. 114 *Small* weak and high-pitched. 115 *babies
lulls asleep* lulls dolls to sleep. *lulls* ROWE; F¹: "lull." 116 *Tent* encamp. *take up*
capture, occupy. 117 *glasses of my sight* my eyeballs. 119-20 *like his . . . an
alms* like that of a beggar bowing in abject gratitude at receiving charity. 121
surcease cease. 123 *inherent* permanent, incapable of eradication. 124-5 *it is
. . . of them* would dishonour me more than it would dishonour you to beg of
them. 126-7 *feel thy . . . stoutness* be injured by (feel the effects of) thy pride
rather than fear the danger caused by your obstinate behaviour (stoutness). This
seems to be the general meaning, although the line is elliptical and obscure. 128
as thou list what you please.

But owe thy pride thyself.

COR.   Pray be content.   130
Mother, I am going to the market place.
Chide me no more. I'll mountebank their loves,
Cog their hearts from them, and come home belov'd
Of all the trades in Rome. Look, I am going.
Commend me to my wife. I'll return consul,   135
Or never trust to what my tongue can do
I' th' way of flattery further.

VOL.   Do your will.   *Exit.*

COM.   Away! The tribunes do attend you. Arm yourself
To answer mildly, for they are prepar'd
With accusations, as I hear, more strong   140
Than are upon you yet.

COR.   The word is "mildly." Pray you let us go.
Let them accuse me by invention; I
Will answer in mine honour.

MEN.   Ay, but mildly.

COR.   Well, mildly be it then — mildly.   *Exeunt.* 145

◇◇◇◇◇◇◇◇◇◇◇◇◇◇◇◇◇

[SCENE III. *Rome. The Forum.*]

Enter Sicinius *and* Brutus.

BRU.   In this point charge him home, that he affects
Tyrannical power. If he evade us there,

---

130 *owe . . . thyself* be the sole owner of your pride.   132 *mountebank their loves* slyly coax their affection from them. A mountebank was a salesman (usually of quack remedies) who operated by trickery.   133 *Cog* wheedle, cheat.   134 *trades* tradesmen.   138 *attend* wait for. *Arm yourself* be prepared.   142 *word* watchword.   143 *by invention* by inventing (charges against me).   144 *in* in accordance with.

    III.III. 1 *charge him home* press the charge against him to the fullest possible extent. *affects* seeks to gain.   2 *there* in that respect.   3 *Enforce him* urge against him strongly. *envy* malice.   4 *on the Antiates* from the citizens of Antium.

Enforce him with his envy to the people,
And that the spoil got on the Antiates
Was ne'er distributed.

Enter an Ædile.

What, will he come?   5

ÆD.   He's coming.

BRU.   How accompanied?

ÆD.   With old Menenius and those senators
That always favour'd him.

SIC.   Have you a catalogue
Of all the voices that we have procur'd
Set down by th' poll?

ÆD.   I have; 'tis ready.   10

SIC.   Have you collected them by tribes?

ÆD.   I have.

SIC.   Assemble presently the people hither;
And when they hear me say "It shall be so
I' th' right and strength o' th' commons," be it either
For death, for fine, or banishment, then let them,   15
If I say fine, cry "Fine!" — if death, cry "Death!"
Insisting on the old prerogative
And power i' th' truth o' th' cause.

ÆD.   I shall inform them.

BRU.   And when such time they have begun to cry,
Let them not cease, but with a din confus'd   20
Enforce the present execution

8–10 *catalogue . . . th' poll* list of all the votes we have procured according to the registry of voters.   11 *tribes* statutory divisions of the Roman populace. Here Shakespeare follows North's Plutarch who says that the Tribunes arranged for the votes to be by "tribes" rather than by the customary "hundreds" so as to give the poor a greater voice than that of the more solid citizens. Actually North, following Amyot, misrepresents Plutarch who pointed out that voting by "hundreds" would have given the Patricians a clear advantage.   12 *presently* at once. 17 *old* customary.   18 *power . . . cause* justice of the case.   19 *when such time* as soon as.   21 *Enforce* insist upon.

Of what we chance to sentence.

ÆD.   Very well.

SIC.   Make them be strong, and ready for this hint
        When we shall hap to give't them.

BRU.   Go about it.

                              [*Exit Ædile.*]

        Put him to choler straight. He hath been us'd   25
        Ever to conquer, and to have his worth
        Of contradiction. Being once chaf'd, he cannot
        Be rein'd again to temperance; then he speaks
        What's in his heart, and that is there which looks
        With us to break his neck.

                    Enter Coriolanus, Menenius, *and* Co-
                    minius, *with others* [*of their party*].

SIC.   Well, here he comes.   30

MEN.   Calmly, I do beseech you.

COR.   Ay, as an hostler, that for th' poorest piece
        Will bear the knave by th' volume. Th' honour'd gods
        Keep Rome in safety, and the chairs of justice
        Supplied with worthy men! plant love among's!   35
        Throng our large temples with the shows of peace
        And not our streets with war!

1. SEN.   Amen, amen.

MEN.   A noble wish.

                    Enter the Ædile, *with the* Plebeians.

SIC.   Draw near, ye people.

ÆD.   List to your tribunes. Audience! Peace, I say!   40

---

24 *hap* happen.   25 *Put . . . straight* anger him at once.   *us'd* accustomed.   26–7
his worth Of contradiction his full share (pennyworth) of power to reply.   27
chaf'd irritated, angered.   28 *rein'd* controlled. The metaphor is from horsemanship.   29–30 *looks . . . neck* gives us the opportunity to break his neck.   32
hostler stable-keeper.   *poorest piece* most worthless coin.   33 *bear the knave* endure insults (being called "knave").   *by th' volume* repeatedly.   36 *Throng* THEO-

COR.   First hear me speak.

BOTH TRIBUNES.   Well, say. Peace, ho!

COR.   Shall I be charg'd no further than this present?
        Must all determine here?

SIC.   I do demand
        If you submit you to the people's voices,
        Allow their officers, and are content   45
        To suffer lawful censure for such faults
        As shall be prov'd upon you.

COR.   I am content.

MEN.   Lo, citizens, he says he is content.
        The warlike service he has done, consider. Think
        Upon the wounds his body bears, which show   50
        Like graves i' th' holy churchyard.

COR.   Scratches with briers,
        Scars to move laughter only.

MEN.   Consider further,
        That when he speaks not like a citizen,
        You find him like a soldier. Do not take
        His rougher accents for malicious sounds,   55
        But, as I say, such as become a soldier
        Rather than envy you.

COM.   [*to* Coriolanus]   Well, well, no more.

COR.   What is the matter,
        That, being pass'd for consul with full voice,
        I am so dishonour'd that the very hour   60
        You take it off again?

SIC.   Answer to us.

BALD; F¹: "Through." *shows* ceremonies, probably festal pageants.   40 *List* listen.
42 *no further . . . present* only at this time (and not again in the future).   43 *determine* be settled.   45 *Allow* acknowledge the authority of.   51 *Like* as deep
and as wide.   52 *move* provoke.   54 *find him like* consider that he is.   55 *accents* manner of speech (THEOBALD; F¹: "Actions").   57 *envy* express malice toward.
59 *pass'd for* elected.   60 *the very hour* at the very same time.

COR.   Say then. 'Tis true, I ought so.

SIC.   We charge you that you have contriv'd to take
  From Rome all season'd office and to wind
  Yourself into a power tyrannical,   65
  For which you are a traitor to the people.

COR.   How? traitor?

MEN.   Nay, temperately! Your promise.

COR.   The fires i' th' lowest hell fold-in the people!
  Call me their traitor, thou injurious tribune?
  Within thine eyes sat twenty thousand deaths, 70
  In thy hands clutch'd as many millions, in
  Thy lying tongue both numbers, I would say
  "Thou liest" unto thee with a voice as free
  As I do pray the gods.

SIC.   Mark you this, people?

ALL [PLEBEIANS]. To th' Rock, to th' Rock with him!

SIC.   Peace! 75
  We need not put new matter to his charge.
  What you have seen him do and heard him speak,
  Beating your officers, cursing yourselves,
  Opposing laws with strokes, and here defying
  Those whose great power must try him — even this, 80
  So criminal and in such capital kind,
  Deserves th' extremest death.

BRU.   But since he hath
  Serv'd well for Rome —

COR.   What do you prate of service?

BRU.   I talk of that that know it.

COR.   You? 85

---

63 *contriv'd* conspired.　64 *season'd office* established offices. *wind* insinuate, work tortuously.　68 *fold-in* encircle.　69 *injurious* insulting, slandering.　70 *Within* if within.　76 *put . . . charge* bring new charges against him.　81 *in such capital kind* of a kind punishable by death.　83 *prate* talk foolishly.　89–90 *pent . . . a day* being imprisoned to slowly starve with but a grain (of food) a

MEN. Is this the promise that you made your mother?

COM. Know, I pray you —

COR.   I'll know no further.
Let them pronounce the steep Tarpeian death,
Vagabond exile, flaying, pent to linger
But with a grain a day — I would not buy   90
Their mercy at the price of one fair word,
Nor check my courage for what they can give,
To have't with saying "Good morrow."

SIC.   For that he has
(As much as in him lies) from time to time
Envied against the people, seeking means   95
To pluck away their power; as now at last
Given hostile strokes, and that not in the presence
Of dreaded justice but on the ministers
That doth distribute it — in the name o' th' people
And in the power of us the tribunes, we   100
(Ev'n from this instant) banish him our city,
In peril of precipitation
From off the Rock Tarpeian, never more
To enter our Rome gates. I' th' people's name,
I say it shall be so.   105

ALL [PLEBEIANS]. It shall be so! it shall be so! Let him away!
He's banish'd, and it shall be so!

COM. Hear me, my masters and my common friends!

SIC. He's sentenc'd. No more hearing.

COM.   Let me speak.
I have been consul, and can show for Rome   110
Her enemies' marks upon me. I do love
My country's good with a respect more tender,
More holy and profound, than mine own life,

---

day.   92 *check* restrain.   93 *with saying* merely by saying.   *For that* because.
94 *as in him lies* as he has been capable of doing.   95 *Envied against* shown
malice toward.   97 *not in* not merely in.   99 *doth* A singular verb with a collective subject is common in Elizabethan English (F¹; F², K: "do").   108 *common*
of lowly station.   110 *show for* THEOBALD; F¹: "show from."

My dear wife's estimate, her womb's increase
And treasure of my loins. Then if I would   115
Speak that —

SIC.   We know your drift. Speak what?

BRU.   There's no more to be said, but he is banish'd,
As enemy to the people and his country.
It shall be so.

ALL [PLEBEIANS].   It shall be so! it shall be so!

COR.   You common cry of curs, whose breath I hate   120
As reek o' th' rotten fens, whose loves I prize
As the dead carcasses of unburied men
That do corrupt my air, I banish you!
And here remain with your uncertainty.
Let every feeble rumour shake your hearts!   125
Your enemies with nodding of their plumes
Fan you into despair! Have the power still
To banish your defenders, till at length
Your ignorance (which finds not till it feels,
Making but reservation of yourselves,   130
Still your own foes) deliver you, as most
Abated captives, to some nation
That won you without blows! Despising
For you the city, thus I turn my back.
There is a world elsewhere.   135

                    Exeunt Coriolanus, Cominius, [Me-
                    nenius,] *with* [*the other* Patricians].

ÆD.   The people's enemy is gone, is gone!

                    *They all shout and throw up their
                    caps.*

ALL.   Our enemy is banish'd! he is gone. Hoo! hoo!

---

114 *estimate* reputation.   114–15 *her womb's . . . loins* my children.   116 *drift*
tenour (of your speech).   120 *cry* pack (a hunting term).   124 *uncertainty* state
of confusion.   126 *plumes* of their helmets.   127 *still* forever.   129 *finds not*
does not learn.   130 *Making . . . yourselves* exempting only yourselves (from

SIC.   Go see him out at gates and follow him
        As he hath follow'd you, with all despite;
        Give him deserv'd vexation. Let a guard   140
        Attend us through the city.

ALL.   Come, come, let's see him out at gates! Come!
        The gods preserve our noble tribunes! Come!   *Exeunt.*

---

banishment) — i.e. you will banish all defenders but your own selves and thus be
left defenceless. *Making but* F¹; CAPELL, K: "Making not."   132 *Abated* humbled.
134 *For you* because of you.   139 *despite* spite.   140 *deserv'd vexation* the tor-
ment he deserves.

Act Four

◇◇

[SCENE I. *Rome. At a gate of the city.*]

Enter Coriolanus, Volumnia, Virgilia, Menenius, Cominius, *with the young* Nobility *of Rome.*

COR. Come, leave your tears. A brief farewell. The beast
With many heads butts me away. Nay, mother,
Where is your ancient courage? You were us'd
To say extremities was the trier of spirits;
That common chances common men could bear;   5
That when the sea was calm, all boats alike
Show'd mastership in floating; fortune's blows
When most struck home, being gentle wounded craves
A noble cunning. You were us'd to load me
With precepts that would make invincible   10
The heart that conn'd them.

VIR.   O heavens! O heavens!

COR.   Nay, I prithee, woman —

VOL. Now the red pestilence strike all trades in Rome,
And occupations perish!

IV.I. 1–2 *The beast . . . heads* A conventional Renaissance characterization of the
fickle populace.   3 *ancient* former.   4 *extremities* F¹; F², K: "extremity." *was*
The singular verb with a collective subject was common in Elizabethan English.
5 *common chances* ordinary vicissitudes of life.   7–9 *fortune's blows . . . cunning*
when fortune's blows strike hardest, to be calm though wounded demands a
knowledge or skill (cunning) appropriate to a gentleman (as opposed to that of
a commoner).   9 *us'd* accustomed.   11 *conn'd* studied.   13 *red pestilence* a
form of the plague characterized by red sores which were regarded as tokens of
death. *trades* tradesmen.   14 *occupations* trades.   15 *lack'd* missed.   22 *salter*

COR.   What, what, what!
          I shall be lov'd when I am lack'd. Nay, mother,   15
          Resume that spirit when you were wont to say,
          If you had been the wife of Hercules,
          Six of his labours you'ld have done, and sav'd
          Your husband so much sweat. Cominius,
          Droop not; adieu. Farewell, my wife, my mother.   20
          I'll do well yet. Thou old and true Menenius,
          Thy tears are salter than a younger man's
          And venomous to thine eyes. My (sometime) General,
          I have seen thee stern, and thou hast oft beheld
          Heart-hard'ning spectacles. Tell these sad women   25
          'Tis fond to wail inevitable strokes,
          As 'tis to laugh at 'em. My mother, you wot well
          My hazards still have been your solace; and
          Believe't not lightly — though I go alone,
          Like to a lonely dragon, that his fen   30
          Makes fear'd and talk'd of more than seen — your son
          Will or exceed the common or be caught
          With cautelous baits and practice.

VOL.   My first son,
          Whither wilt thou go? Take good Cominius
          With thee awhile. Determine on some course   35
          More than a wild exposture to each chance
          That starts i' th' way before thee.

VIR.   O the gods!

COM.   I'll follow thee a month, devise with thee
          Where thou shalt rest, that thou mayst hear of us,
          And we of thee. So, if the time thrust forth   40

---

more salty.   23 *sometime* former.   26 *fond* as foolish.   27 *wot* know.   28
hazards risks (in battle).   *still* always.   29 *not lightly* seriously.   30 *fen* lurking
place. Dragons were believed to inhabit lonely marshes.   31 *Makes . . . seen* i.e.
the loneliness of his fen makes him more often feared than he is seen.   32 *or
. . . common* either be greater than a common man.   33 *cautelous baits* crafty
traps.   *practice* treacherous plots.   *first* first-born.   36 *exposture* exposure.
37 *starts* suddenly appears (a hunting term meaning literally "breaks from
cover").

A cause for thy repeal, we shall not send
O'er the vast world to seek a single man
And lose advantage, which doth ever cool
I' th' absence of the needer.

COR.   Fare ye well.
Thou hast years upon thee, and thou art too full   45
Of the wars' surfeits to go rove with one
That's yet unbruis'd. Bring me but out at gate.
Come, my sweet wife, my dearest mother, and
My friends of noble touch. When I am forth,
Bid me farewell, and smile. I pray you come.   50
While I remain above the ground, you shall
Hear from me still, and never of me aught
But what is like me formerly.

MEN.   That's worthily
As any ear can hear. Come, let's not weep.
If I could shake off but one seven years   55
From these old arms and legs, by the good gods,
I'ld with thee, every foot.

COR.   Give me thy hand.
Come.   *Exeunt.*

◇◇◇◇◇◇◇◇◇◇◇◇◇◇◇◇◇◇

[SCENE II. *Rome. A street near the gate.*]

Enter the two Tribunes, Sicinius *and* Brutus, *with the*
    Ædile.

SIC.   Bid them all home. He's gone, and we'll no further.
        The nobility are vex'd, whom we see have sided

---

41 *repeal* recall from exile.   43 *advantage* opportunity.   45–6 *too full . . . sur-feits* too weak from overindulgence in battle.   47 *yet unbruis'd* Thus Coriolanus lightly dismisses (with the disdain appropriate to an aristocrat) all that he has suffered. *Bring* escort.   49 *of noble touch* who have been truly tested (as a gold coin is tested with a touchstone).   52–3 *aught . . . formerly* Coriolanus has apparently not yet thought of deserting to the Volscians, but the line is ironic in its

In his behalf.

BRU.   Now we have shown our power,
Let us seem humbler after it is done
Than when it was a-doing.

SIC.   Bid them home.   5
Say their great enemy is gone, and they
Stand in their ancient strength.

BRU.   Dismiss them home.
                              [*Exit* Ædile.]
Here comes his mother.

                    Enter Volumnia, Virgilia, *and* Mene-
                    nius.

SIC.   Let's not meet her.

BRU.   Why?

SIC.   They say she's mad.

BRU.   They have ta'en note of us. Keep on your way.   10

VOL.   O, y'are well met. The hoarded plague o' th' gods
Requit your love!

MEN.   Peace, peace! Be not so loud.

VOL.   If that I could for weeping, you should hear —
Nay, and you shall hear some. [*To* Brutus] Will you be
    gone?

VIR.   [*to* Sicinius] You shall stay too. I would I had the power   15
To say so to my husband.

SIC.   Are you mankind?

VOL.   Ay, fool. Is that a shame? Note but this fool!
Was not a man my father? Hadst thou foxship

---

foreshadowing.   53 *worthily* well spoken.
    IV.II. 1 *home* go to their homes.   2 *sided* taken sides.   7 *ancient* former.   11
hoarded stored up.   12 *Requit* repay.   16 *mankind* mad. Volumnia takes it in the
sense of "of the human race."   18 *foxship* craftiness, cunning (the supposed at-
tributes of the fox).

To banish him that struck more blows for Rome
Than thou hast spoken words?

SIC.   O blessed heavens!   20

VOL.   Moe noble blows than ever thou wise words,
And for Rome's good. I'll tell thee what — Yet go!
Nay, but thou shalt stay too. I would my son
Were in Arabia, and thy tribe before him,
His good sword in his hand.

SIC.   What then?

VIR.   What then?   25
He'ld make an end of thy posterity.

VOL.   Bastards and all.
Good man, the wounds that he does bear for Rome!

MEN.   Come, come, peace.

SIC.   I would he had continued to his country   30
As he began, and not unknit himself
The noble knot he made.

BRU.   I would he had.

VOL.   "I would he had"? 'Twas you incens'd the rabble.
Cats, that can judge as fitly of his worth
As I can of those mysteries which heaven   35
Will not have earth to know!

BRU.   Pray let us go.

VOL.   Now, pray, sir, get you gone.
You have done a brave deed. Ere you go, hear this:
As far as doth the Capitol exceed
The meanest house in Rome, so far my son   40
(This lady's husband here, this! Do you see?)
Whom you have banish'd does exceed you all.

BRU.   Well, well, we'll leave you.

---

21 *Moe* more.   24 *Arabia* the desert (where there is no escaping).   31–2 *unknit
. . . he made* himself dissolved the ties of patriotism which bound Rome to him.
35–6 *mysteries . . . to know* That certain knowledge was forbidden to man by
divine injunction was a common Renaissance notion.   38 *brave* fine (used sar-

SIC.   Why stay we to be baited
       With one that wants her wits?   *Exeunt* Tribunes.

VOL.   Take my prayers with you.
       I would the gods had nothing else to do   45
       But to confirm my curses. Could I meet 'em
       But once a day, it would unclog my heart
       Of what lies heavy to't.

MEN.   You have told them home,
       And, by my troth, you have cause. You'll sup with me?

VOL.   Anger's my meat. I sup upon myself,   50
       And so shall starve with feeding. — Come, let's go.
       Leave this faint puling, and lament as I do,
       In anger, Juno-like. Come, come, come!

                       Exeunt [Volumnia *and* Virgilia].

MEN.   Fie, fie, fie!
                                        Exit.

❖❖❖❖❖❖❖❖❖❖❖❖❖❖❖

[SCENE III.
A highway between Rome and Antium.]

Enter a Roman *and a* Volsce [*meeting*].

ROM.   I know you well, sir, and you know me.
       Your name, I think, is Adrian.

VOLSCE.   It is so, sir. Truly I have forgot you.

ROM.   I am a Roman; and my services are, as you are, against
       'em. Know you me yet?   5

VOLSCE.   Nicanor? No?

ROM.   The same, sir.

---

castically). 40 *meanest* lowliest.   44 *wants* lacks.   47 *unclog* remove the weight
(clog) from.   48 *told them home* berated them soundly.   52 *faint puling* weak
whimpering.

VOLSCE.   You had more beard when I last saw you, but your favour is well appear'd by your tongue. What's the news
in Rome? I have a note from the Volscian state to find   10
you out there. You have well saved me a day's journey.

ROM.   There hath been in Rome strange insurrections — the
people against the senators, patricians, and nobles.

VOLSCE.   Hath been? Is it ended then? Our state thinks not so.
They are in a most warlike preparation and hope to   15
come upon them in the heat of their division.

ROM.   The main blaze of it is past, but a small thing would
make it flame again; for the nobles receive so to heart the
banishment of that worthy Coriolanus that they are in a
ripe aptness to take all power from the people and to   20
pluck from them their tribunes for ever. This lies glow-
ing, I can tell you, and is almost mature for the violent
breaking out.

VOLSCE.   Coriolanus banish'd?

ROM.   Banish'd, sir.   25

VOLSCE.   You will be welcome with this intelligence, Nicanor.

ROM.   The day serves well for them now. I have heard it said
the fittest time to corrupt a man's wife is when she's fall'n
out with her husband. Your noble Tullus Aufidius will
appear well in these wars, his great opposer, Coriolanus,   30
being now in no request of his country.

VOLSCE.   He cannot choose. I am most fortunate thus accidentally
to encounter you. You have ended my business, and I
will merrily accompany you home.

ROM.   I shall between this and supper tell you most strange   35
things from Rome, all tending to the good of their ad-

IV.III. 8–9 *favour* face, appearance.   9 *appear'd* rendered apparent, manifested
(F¹; STEEVENS, K: "approv'd").   *tongue* speech. His language reveals that he is a
Roman.   18 *receive* take.   20 *ripe aptness* mature state of readiness.   27 *serves
well* provides a good oportunity.   28–9 *fall'n out* quarrelled.   31 *in no request
of* not required by.   32 *cannot choose* cannot do otherwise (than "appear well").
35 *this* this time.   38 *their charges* men under their command.   38–9 *distinctly*

versaries. Have you an army ready, say you?

VOLSCE. A most royal one, — the centurions and their charges, distinctly billeted, already in th' entertainment and to be on
foot at an hour's warning.   40

ROM. I am joyful to hear of their readiness and am the man, I
think, that shall set them in present action. So, sir, heartily well met, and most glad of your company.

VOLSCE. You take my part from me, sir. I have the most cause to
be glad of yours.   45

ROM. Well, let us go together.   *Exeunt.*

◇◇◇◇◇◇◇◇◇◇◇◇◇◇◇

[SCENE IV. *Antium. Before* Aufidius's *house.*]

Enter Coriolanus *in mean apparel, disguis'd and muffled.*

COR. A goodly city is this Antium. City,
'Tis I that made thy widows. Many an heir
Of these fair edifices fore my wars
Have I heard groan and drop. Then know me not,
Lest that thy wives with spits and boys with stones   5
In puny battle slay me.

Enter a Citizen.

Save you, sir.

CIT. And you.

COR.   Direct me, if it be your will,
Where great Aufidius lies. Is he in Antium?

CIT. He is, and feasts the nobles of the state
At his house this night.

---

billeted individually enrolled (not "assigned to quarters," a different meaning of
the term).   39 *in th' entertainment* entered into the service, engaged to fight.   39–
40 *on foot* marching.   42 *present* immediate.   44 *take . . . me* anticipate my
words; say to me what I should be saying to you.

IV.IV. 3 *fore my wars* facing my onslaught.   6 *puny* petty. *Save* God save.   8
lies dwells.

COR.   Which is his house, beseech you?   10

CIT.   This here before you.

COR.   Thank you, sir. Farewell.

                              Exit Citizen.

O world, thy slippery turns! Friends now fast sworn,
Whose double bosom seems to wear one heart,
Whose hours, whose bed, whose meal and exercise
Are still together, who twin (as 'twere) in love   15
Unseparable, shall within this hour,
On a dissension of a doit, break out
To bitterest enmity. So fellest foes,
Whose passions and whose plots have broke their sleep
To take the one the other, by some chance,   20
Some trick not worth an egg, shall grow dear friends
And interjoin their issues. So with me.
My birthplace hate I, and my love 's upon
This enemy town. I'll enter. If he slay me,
He does fair justice; if he give me way,   25
I'll do his country service.   *Exit.*

◇◇◇◇◇◇◇◇◇◇◇◇◇◇◇◇

[SCENE V. *Antium. A hall in* Aufidius's *house.*]

Music plays. Enter a Servingman.

1. SERV.   Wine, wine, wine! What service is here! I think our fel-
           lows are asleep.   [*Exit.*]

              Enter another Servingman.

---

12 *slippery turns* fickle changes of fortune.   13 *Whose . . . heart* whose two
bodies seem to contain but a single heart (a traditional description of true friendship).   15 *still* always.   17 *On . . . doit* because of a very trivial dispute. A
"doit" was a coin of very slight value.   18 *fellest* fiercest.   19–20 *Whose passions
. . . the other* who have been kept awake at night by their hatred and their
plotting to get the better of one another.   21 *trick* trivial matter.   22 *interjoin*

2. SERV.	Where's Cotus? My master calls for him. Cotus! *Exit.*

Enter Coriolanus.

COR.	A goodly house. The feast smells well, but I	
	Appear not like a guest.	5

Enter the first Servingman.

1. SERV.	What would you have, friend? Whence are you? Here's no place for you. Pray go to the door. *Exit.*
COR.	I have deserv'd no better entertainment In being Coriolanus.

Enter second Servant.

2. SERV.	Whence are you, sir? Has the porter his eyes in his head that he gives entrance to such companions? Pray get you out.	10
COR.	Away!	
2. SERV.	Away? Get you away!	
COR.	Now th'art troublesome.	15
2. SERV.	Are you so brave? I'll have you talk'd with anon.	

Enter third Servingman; *the first meets him.*

3. SERV.	What fellow 's this?
1. SERV.	A strange one as ever I look'd on. I cannot get him out o' th' house. Prithee call my master to him.

3. SERV.	What have you to do here, fellow? Pray you avoid the house.	20
COR.	Let me but stand. I will not hurt your hearth.	

---

their issues (a) cause their children to marry one another (b) make common cause with one another. Either or both meanings may have been intended. **23** *hate I* CAPELL; F¹: "haue I." **25** *give me way* accede to my wishes.

    IV.v. **1–2** *fellows* fellow servants. **5** *Appear not* am not dressed. **8** *entertainment* reception. **11** *companions* rascals. **16** *brave* insolent. **20** *avoid* depart from.

3. SERV.	What are you?
COR.	A gentleman.
3. SERV.	A marv'llous poor one.	25
COR.	True, so I am.

3. SERV.   Pray you, poor gentleman, take up some other station. Here's no place for you. Pray you avoid. Come.

COR.   Follow your function, go and batten on cold bits.

Pushes him away from him.

3. SERV.   What, you will not? Prithee tell my master what a   30
strange guest he has here.

2. SERV.   And I shall.   *Exit.*

3. SERV.   Where dwell'st thou?

COR.   Under the canopy.

3. SERV.   Under the canopy?   35

COR.   Ay.

3. SERV.   Where's that?

COR.   I' th' city of kites and crows.

3. SERV.   I' th' city of kites and crows? What an ass it is! — Then
thou dwell'st with daws too?   40

COR.   No, I serve not thy master.

3. SERV.   How, sir? Do you meddle with my master?

COR.   Ay. 'Tis an honester service than to meddle with thy
mistress.
Thou prat'st and prat'st. Serve with thy trencher. Hence! 45

Beats him away.

Enter Aufidius, *with the* [*second*]
Servingman.

---

25 *marv'llous* strangely.   29 *Follow your function* do your customary work.
batten grow fat.   34 *canopy* sky (a common metaphor).   40 *daws* jackdaws,
known for their foolish chattering.   43 *honester* (a) more honourable (b) more
chaste.   43 *meddle with* (a) be involved with (b) have sexual relations with.   45

AUF.   Where is this fellow?

2. SERV.   Here, sir. I'd have beaten him like a dog but for disturbing the lords within.

> [*While* Aufidius *and* Coriolanus *con-*
> *verse, the first and second* Servingmen
> *stand back.*]

AUF.   Whence com'st thou? What wouldst thou? Thy name?
Why speak'st not? Speak, man. What's thy name?

COR.   If, Tullus,   [*Unmuffles.*]   50
Not yet thou know'st me, and, seeing me, dost not
Think me for the man I am, necessity
Commands me name myself.

AUF.   What is thy name?

COR.   A name unmusical to the Volscians' ears
And harsh in sound to thine.

AUF.   Say, what's thy name?   55
Thou hast a grim appearance, and thy face
Bears a command in't. Though thy tackle 's torn,
Thou show'st a noble vessel. What's thy name?

COR.   Prepare thy brow to frown. Know'st thou me yet?

AUF.   I know thee not. Thy name?   60

COR.   My name is Caius Marcius, who hath done
To thee particularly and to all the Volsces
Great hurt and mischief. Thereto witness may
My surname Coriolanus. The painful service,
The extreme dangers, and the drops of blood   65
Shed for my thankless country are requitted
But with that surname — a good memory
And witness of the malice and displeasure
Which thou shouldst bear me. Only that name remains.

---

prat'st talk foolishly. *trencher* wooden dish.   47–8 *but for disturbing* except
that it (my beating him) would disturb.   52 *Think* recognize.   57 *Bears . . .*
in't has a commanding look. *tackle* rigging of a vessel.   66 *are requitted* have
been rewarded.   67 *memory* memorial.

The cruelty and envy of the people,   70
Permitted by our dastard nobles, who
Have all forsook me, hath devour'd the rest
And suffer'd me by th' voice of slaves to be
Whoop'd out of Rome. Now this extremity
Hath brought me to thy hearth; not out of hope   75
(Mistake me not) to save my life; for if
I had fear'd death, of all the men i' th' world
I would have 'voided thee; but in mere spite,
To be full quit of those my banishers,
Stand I before thee here. Then if thou hast   80
A heart of wreak in thee, that wilt revenge
Thine own particular wrongs and stop those maims
Of shame seen through thy country, speed thee straight
And make my misery serve thy turn. So use it
That my revengeful services may prove   85
As benefits to thee; for I will fight
Against my cank'red country with the spleen
Of all the under fiends. But if so be
Thou dar'st not this, and that to prove more fortunes
Th'art tir'd, then, in a word, I also am   90
Longer to live most weary, and present
My throat to thee and to thy ancient malice;
Which not to cut would show thee but a fool,
Since I have ever followed thee with hate,
Drawn tuns of blood out of thy country's breast,   95
And cannot live but to thy shame, unless
It be to do thee service.

AUF.   O Marcius, Marcius!
Each word thou hast spoke hath weeded from my heart

---

70 *envy* malice.   71 *dastard* cowardly.   73 *suffer'd* caused.   74 *Whoop'd* chased
with shouts.   78 *'voided* avoided.   *in mere* entirely in.   79 *be full quit of* fully
settle my account with.   81 *of wreak* full of desire for vengeance.   82–3 *stop
. . . shame* end those ignominious mutilations.   83 *through* throughout.   *speed
thee straight* hasten at once.   87 *cank'red* diseased, corrupted.   *spleen* anger.   88
under fiends infernal fiends.   89 *prove* try.   95 *tuns* barrels. The image is that
of wine casks being tapped.   96–7 *And cannot . . . service* my living can only
be a shame to you, unless by living I can do you a service.   104 *grained ash*
spear shaft made of stout ash.   105 *scarr'd* Some editors have read "scar'd." In
either case, we have an extravagant hyperbole.   *clip* embrace, clasp (POPE; F¹, K:

A root of ancient envy. If Jupiter
Should from yond cloud speak divine things   100
And say " 'Tis true," I'd not believe them more
Than thee, all-noble Marcius. Let me twine
Mine arms about that body whereagainst
My grained ash an hundred times hath broke
And scarr'd the moon with splinters. Here I clip   105
The anvil of my sword, and do contest
As hotly and as nobly with thy love
As ever in ambitious strength I did
Contend against thy valour. Know thou first,
I lov'd the maid I married; never man   110
Sigh'd truer breath. But that I see thee here,
Thou noble thing, more dances my rapt heart
Than when I first my wedded mistress saw
Bestride my threshold. Why, thou Mars, I tell thee
We have a power on foot, and I had purpose   115
Once more to hew thy target from thy brawn
Or lose mine arm for't. Thou hast beat me out
Twelve several times, and I have nightly since
Dreamt of encounters 'twixt thyself and me —
We have been down together in my sleep,   120
Unbuckling helms, fisting each other's throat —
And wak'd half dead with nothing. Worthy Marcius,
Had we no other quarrel else to Rome but that
Thou art thence banish'd, we would muster all
From twelve to seventy, and, pouring war   125
Into the bowels of ungrateful Rome,
Like a bold flood o'erbeat. O, come, go in,
And take our friendly senators by th' hands,

"cleep").   106 *anvil of my sword* i.e. Coriolanus, called an anvil because upon
him his sword has struck heavy blows.   111 *Sigh'd truer breath* made his prot-
estations of love more honestly.   112 *dances . . . heart* causes my enraptured
heart to dance.   114 *Bestride* step across.   115 *a power on foot* an army assem-
bled.   116 *target* small shield worn on the arm. *brawn* muscular arm.   117
out thoroughly.   120 *down together* grappling on the ground.   121 *helms* helmets. *fisting* clutching.   127 *o'erbeat* sweep over and destroy. Some editors read
"o'erbear" or "o'erbear't," words more commonly used by Shakespeare in connec-
tion with floods.

Who now are here, taking their leaves of me
Who am prepar'd against your territories,   130
Though not for Rome itself.

COR.   You bless me, gods!

AUF.   Therefore, most absolute sir, if thou wilt have
The leading of thine own revenges, take
Th' one half of my commission, and set down —
As best thou art experienc'd, since thou know'st   135
Thy country's strength and weakness — thine own ways,
Whether to knock against the gates of Rome,
Or rudely visit them in parts remote
To fright them ere destroy. But come in.
Let me commend thee first to those that shall   140
Say yea to thy desires. A thousand welcomes!
And more a friend than e'er an enemy.
Yet, Marcius, that was much. Your hand. Most welcome!

> *Exeunt* [Coriolanus *and* Aufidius].
>
> *Two of the* Servingmen, [*the first and second, come forward*].

1. SERV.   Here's a strange alteration!

2. SERV.   By my hand, I had thought to have stroken him with a   145
cudgel — and yet my mind gave me his clothes made a
false report of him.

1. SERV.   What an arm he has! He turn'd me about with his finger
and his thumb as one would set up a top.

2. SERV.   Nay, I knew by his face that there was something in   150
him. He had, sir, a kind of face, methought — I cannot
tell how to term it.

1. SERV.   He had so, looking as it were — Would I were hang'd
but I thought there was more in him than I could think.

---

130 *am prepar'd* have an army in readiness.   132 *absolute* perfect, without defect.
134 *my commission* the troops under my command.   *set down* decide, establish
as the order of battle.   138 *visit* attack.   140 *commend* introduce.   141 *desires*
orders.   145 *stroken* struck.   146 *my mind gave me* I suspected.   157 *wot on*
know of.   160 *on* of.   171 *wont* accustomed.   178 *directly* in face-to-face com-

2. SERV.   So did I, I'll be sworn. He is simply the rarest man i' th'   155
world.

1. SERV.   I think he is; but a greater soldier than he you wot on.

2. SERV.   Who? My master?

1. SERV.   Nay, it's no matter for that.

2. SERV.   Worth six on him.   160

1. SERV.   Nay, not so neither. But I take him to be the greater
soldier.

2. SERV.   Faith, look you, one cannot tell how to say that. For the
defence of a town our general is excellent.

1. SERV.   Ay, and for an assault too.   165

Enter the third Servingman.

3. SERV.   O slaves, I can tell you news! news, you rascals!

BOTH 1. AND 2. SERV. What, what, what? Let's partake.

3. SERV.   I would not be a Roman, of all nations. I had as lief be
a condemn'd man.

BOTH.   Wherefore? wherefore?   170

3. SERV.   Why, here's he that was wont to thwack our general —
Caius Marcius.

1. SERV.   Why do you say "thwack our general"?

3. SERV.   I do not say "thwack our general," but he was always
good enough for him.   175

2. SERV.   Come, we are fellows and friends. He was ever too hard
for him. I have heard him say so himself.

1. SERV.   He was too hard for him directly, to say the troth on't.
Before Corioles he scotch'd him and notch'd him like a
carbonado.   180

2. SERV.   An he had been cannibally given, he might have boil'd
and eaten him too.

---

bat. *troth on't* truth about it.   179 *scotch'd* slashed.   180 *carbonado* cut of
meat prepared for cooking.   181 *given* inclined. *boil'd* F¹; POPE, K: "broil'd."
The emendation rests upon the assumption that a carbonado is usually broiled
rather than boiled, but we have no reason to suppose that Shakespeare in a
conversation between servants would be so meticulous about culinary details.

1. SERV. But more of thy news!

3. SERV. Why, he is so made on here within as if he were son
          and heir to Mars; set at upper end o' th' table; no   185
          question ask'd him by any of the senators but they stand
          bald before him. Our general himself makes a mistress
          of him, sanctifies himself with 's hand and turns up the
          white o' th' eye to his discourse. But the bottom of the
          news is, our general is cut i' th' middle and but one half   190
          of what he was yesterday, for the other has half by the
          entreaty and grant of the whole table. He'll go, he says,
          and sole the porter of Rome gates by th' ears. He will
          mow all down before him and leave his passage poll'd.

2. SERV. And he's as like to do't as any man I can imagine.   195

3. SERV. Do't? He will do't; for look you, sir, he has as many
          friends as enemies; which friends, sir, as it were, durst
          not (look you, sir) show themselves (as we term it) his
          friends whilst he's in directitude.

1. SERV. Directitude? What's that?   200

3. SERV. But when they shall see, sir, his crest up again and the
          man in blood, they will out of their burrows, like conies
          after rain, and revel all with him.

1. SERV. But when goes this forward?

3. SERV. To-morrow, to-day, presently. You shall have the drum   205
          struck up this afternoon. 'Tis as it were a parcel of their
          feast, and to be executed ere they wipe their lips.

2. SERV. Why, then we shall have a stirring world again. This
          peace is nothing but to rust iron, increase tailors, and

---

184 *made on* fussed over.   187 *bald* bareheaded.   188 *sanctifies . . . hand* treats
the touch of his hand as a holy blessing (as though he were his mistress being
courted).   188–9 *turns up . . . discourse* listens to his speech with an expression
of piety.   189 *bottom* final item.   190–2 *our general . . . whole table*. The point
is that there are now two generals, Coriolanus being afforded an equal position
with Aufidius by consent of all the senators.   193 *sole* drag roughly.   194 *poll'd*
cleared. To "poll" trees was to crop them, clearing away the dead branches.   195
like likely.   199 *directitude* The meaning has been much disputed, but the word
is most likely to be a deliberate servant's blunder for "discredit."   220 *his crest
up again* his pride reasserted. The "crest" was a traditional symbol of pride.

breed ballad-makers. 210

1. SERV. Let me have war, say I. It exceeds peace as far as day
does night. It's sprightly, waking, audible, and full of
vent. Peace is a very apoplexy, lethargy; mull'd, deaf,
sleepy, insensible; a getter of more bastard children than
war's a destroyer of men. 215

2. SERV. 'Tis so; and as war in some sort may be said to be a
ravisher, so it cannot be denied but peace is a great
maker of cuckolds.

1. SERV. Ay, and it makes men hate one another.

3. SERV. Reason; because they then less need one another. The 220
wars for my money! I hope to see Romans as cheap as
Volscians. They are rising, they are rising.

BOTH [1. AND 2. SERV.]. In, in, in, in! *Exeunt.*

❖❖❖❖❖❖❖❖❖❖❖❖❖

[SCENE VI. *Rome. A public place.*]

Enter the two Tribunes, Sicinius *and* Brutus.

SIC. We hear not of him, neither need we fear him:
His remedies are tame. The present peace
And quietness of the people, which before
Were in wild hurry here, do make his friends
Blush that the world goes well; who rather had, 5
Though they themselves did suffer by't, behold
Dissentious numbers pest'ring streets than see
Our tradesmen singing in their shops and going

---

202 *in blood* in full vigour (a term usually applied to hounds). *conies* rabbits.
204 *goes this forward* is this to take place. 205 *presently* at once. 206 *parcel*
part. 208 *stirring* active. 212 *sprightly* full of spirit. *waking* wide-awake,
alert (POPE; F¹: "walking"). *audible* full of noise. 213 *vent* scent. War is being
compared to a hunting dog, alert and barking as it tracks down its prey. 213
apoplexy state of paralysis. *mull'd* warm and drowsy. 214 *sleepy* F³; F¹:
"sleepe." *getter* begetter. 216 *war* ROWE; F¹: "warres." 222 *rising* from the table.
IV.VI. 2 *His remedies are tame* his means of redress (against us) are ineffectual.
7 *pest'ring* creating disturbances in.

	About their functions friendly.
BRU.	We stood to 't in good time.

Enter Menenius.

Is this Menenius?   10

SIC.	'Tis he, 'tis he! O, he is grown most kind
	Of late. — Hail, sir!
MEN.	Hail to you both!
SIC.	Your Coriolanus is not much miss'd
	But with his friends. The commonwealth doth stand,
	And so would do, were he more angry at it. 15
MEN.	All's well, and might have been much better if
	He could have temporiz'd.
SIC.	Where is he, hear you?
MEN.	Nay, I hear nothing. His mother and his wife
	Hear nothing from him.

Enter three or four Citizens.

ALL [CITIZENS].	The gods preserve you both!
SIC.	Good-en, our neighbours. 20
BRU.	Good-en to you all, good-en to you all.
1. CIT.	Ourselves, our wives, and children, on our knees
	Are bound to pray for you both.
SIC.	Live and thrive!
BRU.	Farewell, kind neighbours. We wish'd Coriolanus
	Had lov'd you as we did.
ALL [CITIZENS].	Now the gods keep you! 25
BOTH TRIB.	Farewell, farewell. *Exeunt* Citizens.
SIC.	This is a happier and more comely time
	Than when these fellows ran about the streets

10 *stood to 't* took a firm position.   14 *But with* except by.   17 *temporiz'd* compromised, come to terms.   20 *Good-en* good evening.   27 *comely* decorous.
32–3 *affecting . . . assistance* desiring to rule alone, without partners.   34 *by*

Crying confusion.

BRU.   Caius Marcius was
A worthy officer i' th' war, but insolent,   30
O'ercome with pride, ambitious past all thinking,
Self-loving —

SIC.   And affecting one sole throne
Without assistance.

MEN.   I think not so.

SIC.   We should by this, to all our lamentation,
If he had gone forth consul, found it so.   35

BRU.   The gods have well prevented it, and Rome
Sits safe and still without him.

Enter an Ædile.

ÆD.   Worthy tribune,
There is a slave whom we have put in prison
Reports the Volsces with two several powers
Are ent'red in the Roman territories   40
And with the deepest malice of the war
Destroy what lies before 'em.

MEN.   'Tis Aufidius,
Who, hearing of our Marcius' banishment,
Thrusts forth his horns again into the world,
Which were inshell'd when Marcius stood for Rome,   45
And durst not once peep out.

SIC.   Come, what talk you of Marcius?

BRU.   Go see this rumourer whipp'd. It cannot be
The Volsces dare break with us.

MEN.   Cannot be?
We have record that very well it can,
And three examples of the like hath been   50

this by this time.   39 *several powers* separate armies.   44 *Thrusts . . . horns*
The metaphor is that of a snail.   45 *inshell'd* enclosed within his (the snail's)
shell.   48 *break* break faith.

Within my age. But reason with the fellow
Before you punish him, where he heard this,
Lest you shall chance to whip your information
And beat the messenger who bids beware
Of what is to be dreaded.

SIC.   Tell not me.   55
I know this cannot be.

BRU.   Not possible.

Enter a Messenger.

MESS.   The nobles in great earnestness are going
All to the Senate House. Some news is come
That turns their countenances.

SIC.   'Tis this slave —
Go whip him fore the people's eyes! — his raising,   60
Nothing but his report.

MESS.   Yes, worthy sir.
The slave's report is seconded, and more,
More fearful, is deliver'd.

SIC.   What more fearful?

MESS.   It is spoke freely out of many mouths
(How probable I do not know) that Marcius,   65
Join'd with Aufidius, leads a power 'gainst Rome
And vows revenge as spacious as between
The young'st and oldest thing.

SIC.   This is most likely!

BRU.   Rais'd only that the weaker sort may wish
Good Marcius home again.

SIC.   The very trick on't.   70

---

51 *age* lifetime. *reason* discuss.   53 *information* source of information.   58
come ROWE; F¹: "comming."   59 *turns* (a) changes (b) turns sour — as milk is
said to "turn."   60 *fore* before. *raising* invention (of the rumour).   62 *seconded*
supported.   63 *deliver'd* reported.   66 *power* army.   67–8 *as spacious . . .
thing* so all-encompassing that he will spare neither young nor old.   69 *Rais'd*
invented.   72 *atone* come to terms.   73 *violent'st contrariety* the most violent
by the bore of an augur.   93 *brats* contemptible and insignificant creatures.

MEN.   This is unlikely.
        He and Aufidius can no more atone
        Than violent'st contrariety.

                Enter [another] Messenger.

MESS.   You are sent for to the Senate.
        A fearful army, led by Caius Marcius   75
        Associated with Aufidius, rages
        Upon our territories, and have already
        O'erborne their way, consum'd with fire and took
        What lay before them.

                Enter Cominius.

COM.   O, you have made good work!

MEN.   What news? What news?   80

COM.   You have holp to ravish your own daughters and
        To melt the city leads upon your pates,
        To see your wives dishonour'd to your noses —

MEN.   What's the news? What's the news?

COM.   Your temples burned in their cement, and   85
        Your franchises, whereon you stood, confin'd
        Into an auger's bore.

MEN.   Pray now, your news!
        You have made fair work, I fear me. Pray, your news!
        If Marcius should be join'd with Volscians —

COM.   If?
        He is their god. He leads them like a thing   90
        Made by some other deity than Nature,
        That shapes man better; and they follow him
        Against us brats with no less confidence

---

opposites.   78 *O'erborne their way* overwhelmed all opposition.   81 *holp*
helped.   82 *To melt . . . pates* to cause the melting lead from the roofs of burning houses to fall upon your heads.   83 *to your noses* before your faces.   86
franchises political rights. *whereon you stood* upon which you insisted.   86–7
confin'd . . . bore made as small as what may be enclosed in the smallest hole,
that made by the bore of an augur.   93 *brats* contemptible and insignificant
creatures.

Than boys pursuing summer butterflies
Or butchers killing flies.

MEN.   You have made good work,   95
You and your apron-men! you that stood so much
Upon the voice of occupation and
The breath of garlic-eaters!

COM.   He will shake
Your Rome about your ears.

MEN.   As Hercules
Did shake down mellow fruit. You have made fair work!   100

BRU.   But is this true, sir?

COM.   Ay, and you'll look pale
Before you find it other. All the regions
Do smilingly revolt, and who resists
Are mock'd for valiant ignorance
And perish constant fools. Who is't can blame him?   105
Your enemies and his find something in him.

MEN.   We are all undone unless
The noble man have mercy.

COM.   Who shall ask it?
The tribunes cannot do't for shame. The people
Deserve such pity of him as the wolf   110
Does of the shepherds. For his best friends, if they
Should say "Be good to Rome," they charg'd him even
As those should do that had deserv'd his hate,
And therein show'd like enemies.

MEN.   'Tis true.
If he were putting to my house the brand   115
That should consume it, I have not the face

---

95 *butchers killing flies* The havoc made by butchers among flies was proverbial.
96 *apron-men* tradesmen (who wore aprons). *stood* insisted.   97 *voice of occupation* right of working men to vote.   98 *breath* voices, votes.   100 *mellow fruit* the golden apples of the Hesperides attained by Hercules as his eleventh labour.
103 *resists* F¹; HANMER, K: "resist."   105 *constant fools* (a) foolishly loyal (b) constant in their folly.   107 *undone* ruined.   112 *charg'd* would be enjoining.
114 *show'd* would appear.   116 *face* effrontery.   117 *fair hands* good work

To say "Beseech you cease." You have made fair hands,
You and your crafts! You have crafted fair!

COM.   You have brought
A trembling upon Rome, such as was never
S' incapable of help.

TRIBUNES.   Say not we brought it.   120

MEN. How? Was it we? We lov'd him, but, like beasts
And cowardly nobles, gave way unto your clusters,
Who did hoot him out o' th' city.

COM.   But I fear
They'll roar him in again. Tullus Aufidius,
The second name of men, obeys his points   125
As if he were his officer. Desperation
Is all the policy, strength, and defence
That Rome can make against them.

Enter a troop of Citizens.

MEN.   Here come the clusters.
And is Aufidius with him? You are they
That made the air unwholesome when you cast   130
Your stinking greasy caps in hooting at
Coriolanus' exile. Now he's coming,
And not a hair upon a soldier's head
Which will not prove a whip. As many coxcombs
As you threw caps up will he tumble down   135
And pay you for your voices. 'Tis no matter.
If he could burn us all into one coal,
We have deserv'd it.

OMNES. Faith, we hear fearful news.

1. CIT.   For mine own part,
When I said banish him, I said 'twas pity.   140

(sarcastically).   118 *crafts* (a) tradesmen (b) trickery. *crafted fair* made a fine job
of it.   119 *trembling* fit of fear.   120 *S' incapable* so incapable.   122 *clusters*
crowds.   124 *roar him* cry to him for mercy.   125 *The second name of men* whose
fame (as a fighter) is second among all men (the first being Coriolanus). *his
points* Coriolanus' directions.   126 *officer* lieutenant, subordinate.   128 *make*
muster.   134 *coxcombs* heads of fools.   136 *pay* repay, punish.

2. CIT.	And so did I.
3. CIT.	And so did I; and, to say the truth, so did very many of us. That we did, we did for the best; and though we willingly consented to his banishment, yet it was against our will. 145
COM.	Y'are goodly things, you voices!
MEN.	You have made Good work, you and your cry! Shall's to the Capitol?
COM.	O, ay! What else? *Exeunt both.*
SIC.	Go, masters, get you home. Be not dismay'd. These are a side that would be glad to have 150 This true which they so seem to fear. Go home And show no sign of fear.
1. CIT.	The gods be good to us! Come, masters, let's home. I ever said we were i' th' wrong when we banish'd him.
2. CIT.	So did we all. But come, let's home. *Exeunt* Citizens. 155
BRU.	I do not like this news.
SIC.	Nor I.
BRU.	Let's to the Capitol. Would half my wealth Would buy this for a lie!
SIC.	Pray let us go.
	Exeunt Tribunes.

❖❖❖❖❖❖❖❖❖❖❖❖❖❖

[SCENE VII.
A camp, at a short distance from Rome.]

Enter Aufidius *with his* Lieutenant.

143 *That* what.   147 *cry* pack (of dogs).   *Shall's* shall we go.   158–9 *Would . . . lie* I would give half my wealth to have this news prove false.

IV.VII. 3 *fore* before.   5 *dark'ned* obscured, rendered less bright.   6 *your own* your own men. Some have suggested that it may refer to "your own action (in making him commander)."   7 *using means* resorting to means by which.   11 *changeling* a child substituted by fairies for one they have stolen. To be "no

AUF.   Do they still fly to th' Roman?

LIEUT.   I do not know what witchcraft 's in him, but
          Your soldiers use him as the grace fore meat,
          Their talk at table, and their thanks at end;
          And you are dark'ned in this action, sir,   5
          Even by your own.

AUF.   I cannot help it now,
          Unless by using means I lame the foot
          Of our design. He bears himself more proudlier,
          Even to my person, than I thought he would
          When first I did embrace him. Yet his nature   10
          In that's no changeling, and I must excuse
          What cannot be amended.

LIEUT.   Yet I wish, sir
          (I mean for your particular), you had not
          Join'd in commission with him; but either
          Had borne the action of yourself, or else   15
          To him had left it solely.

AUF.   I understand thee well; and be thou sure,
          When he shall come to his account, he knows not
          What I can urge against him. Although it seems,
          And so he thinks, and is no less apparent   20
          To th' vulgar eye, that he bears all things fairly
          And shows good husbandry for the Volscian state,
          Fights dragon-like, and does achieve as soon
          As draw his sword; yet he hath left undone
          That which shall break his neck or hazard mine   25
          Whene'er we come to our account.

---

changeling" is thus to be constant and unswerving.   13 *your particular* that
which especially concerns you.   15 *Had* POPE; F¹: "haue." *of yourself* by yourself.   19 *urge against him* charge him with.   21 *vulgar eye* eyes of the common
people.   22 *husbandry* management.   23 *dragon-like* To fight like a dragon
seems to have been a proverbial expression for to fight savagely but alone.
achieve gain success.

LIEUT.   Sir, I beseech you, think you he'll carry Rome?

AUF.   All places yield to him ere he sits down,
         And the nobility of Rome are his;
         The senators and patricians love him too.   30
         The tribunes are no soldiers, and their people
         Will be as rash in the repeal as hasty
         To expel him thence. I think he'll be to Rome
         As is the osprey to the fish, who takes it
         By sovereignty of nature. First he was   35
         A noble servant to them, but he could not
         Carry his honours even. Whether 'twas pride,
         Which out of daily fortune ever taints
         The happy man; whether defect of judgment,
         To fail in the disposing of those chances   40
         Which he was lord of; or whether nature,
         Not to be other than one thing, not moving
         From th' casque to th' cushion, but commanding peace
         Even with the same austerity and garb
         As he controll'd the war; but one of these   45
         (As he hath spices of them all, not all,
         For I dare so far free him) made him fear'd,
         So hated, and so banish'd. But he has a merit
         To choke it in the utt'rance. So our virtues
         Lie in th' interpretation of the time;   50
         And power, unto itself most commendable,
         Hath not a tomb so evident as a chair
         T' extol what it hath done.

---

27 *carry* conquer.   28 *places* fortified positions.   *yield* F²; F¹: "yeelds."   *sits down*
lays siege.   29 *are his* are already on his side.   32 *rash in the repeal* hasty in
recalling him (from exile).   34 *osprey* hawk trained to catch fish which supposedly
were dazzled by its white underbelly as it flew over the water.   *takes it* captures
it (the fish).   35 *sovereignty of nature* natural superiority.   36 *them* the
Romans.   37 *Carry . . . even* bear the honours heaped upon him without losing
his own sense of balance.   38-9 *Which out . . . happy man* which arising out of
continued success always corrupts the prosperous man.   39 *defect* F²; F¹: "detect."
40-1 *the disposing . . . lord of* properly using those opportunities which came
his way.   41-2 *nature . . . one thing* a character which made him incapable of
playing more than a single role.   42-3 *not moving . . . cushion* incapable of
moving from warlike behaviour (casque) to the exercising of authority in time
of peace. The "cushion" was the seat of a senator.   44 *garb* manner.   45 *con-*

One fire drives out one fire; one nail, one nail;
Rights by rights falter, strengths by strengths do fail.   55
Come, let 's away. When, Caius, Rome is thine,
Thou art poor'st of all; then shortly art thou mine.

Exeunt.

---

troll'd commanded in.   *but one* merely one.   46 *hath spices . . . not all* has
some part of each (of these defects) but none of them entirely.   47 *so far free
him* absolve him to that extent.   48 *So* therefore.   48–9 *a merit . . . utt'rance*
that kind of merit which is vitiated as soon as it is expressed (made evident).
49 *virtues* F²; F¹: "vertue."   50 *the time* our fellow men.   51–3 *And power . . .
hath done* and a powerful man, conscious of his own worth, has no means of
destroying himself more obvious than a public rostrum (chair) from which he
praises what his own power has accomplished. This seems to be the general
meaning of this complex and difficult sentence.   54 *One fire . . . one nail* These
are old proverbs, the point of which is that any quality has the power of
destroying itself.   55 *falter* DYCE; F¹: "fouler." Some editors read "founder."
57 *shortly* soon afterwards.

Act Five

◇◇

[SCENE I. *Rome. A public place.*]

Enter Menenius, Cominius; Sicinius, Brutus, *the two*
Tribunes; *with others.*

MEN.   No, I'll not go. You hear what he hath said
Which was sometime his general, who lov'd him
In a most dear particular. He call'd me father.
But what o' that? Go you that banish'd him;
A mile before his tent fall down, and knee   5
The way into his mercy. Nay, if he coy'd
To hear Cominius speak, I'll keep at home.

COM.   He would not seem to know me.

MEN.   Do you hear?

COM.   Yet one time he did call me by my name.
I urg'd our old acquaintance, and the drops   10
That we have bled together. Coriolanus
He would not answer to; forbade all names.
He was a kind of nothing, titleless,

V.I. 2 *Which* who. *sometime* formerly.　3 *In a most dear particular* with a very close personal affection. There is a quibble on "general" of which "particular" is the exact opposite.　5 *knee* crawl. There is a glance at the practice of pilgrims crawling up to a shrine.　6 *coy'd* was reluctant.　7 *keep* stay.　8 *seem to know* give any sign of knowing.　10 *urg'd* offered as an argument.　16 *rack'd for* exerted themselves in order for (POPE; F¹: "wrack'd for": K: "wrack'd fair"). This reading has been much disputed. Some editors read "wreck'd fair."　17 *memory*

Till he had forg'd himself a name i' th' fire
Of burning Rome.

MEN.   Why, so! You have made good work? 15
A pair of tribunes that have rack'd for Rome
To make coals cheap! A noble memory!

COM. I minded him how royal 'twas to pardon
When it was less expected. He replied,
It was a bare petition of a state   20
To one whom they had punish'd.

MEN.   Very well.
Could he say less?

COM. I offered to awaken his regard
For 's private friends. His answer to me was,
He could not stay to pick them in a pile   25
Of noisome musty chaff. He said 'twas folly,
For one poor grain or two, to leave unburnt
And still to nose th' offence.

MEN.   For one poor grain or two?
I am one of those! his mother, wife, his child,
And this brave fellow too — we are the grains;   30
You are the musty chaff, and you are smelt
Above the moon. We must be burnt for you!

SIC. Nay, pray be patient. If you refuse your aid
In this so never-needed help, yet do not
Upbraid 's with our distress. But sure, if you   35
Would be your country's pleader, your good tongue,
More than the instant army we can make,
Might stop our countryman.

MEN.   No, I'll not meddle.

---

memorial.   18 *minded* reminded.   20 *a bare* merely a.   23 *offered* attempted.
25 *stay* stop.   25–6 *to pick . . . chaff* The metaphor is that of the winnowing of
grain.   *noisome* disgusting, offensive to the smell.   28 *nose th' offence* smell the
offensive stuff.   30 *brave* fine.   32 *Above the moon* A typical hyperbole — like "to
high heaven."   34 *so never-needed help* situation where help is needed as never
before.   37 *the instant . . . make* any army we can raise on such short notice.

SIC. Pray you go to him.

MEN.   What should I do?

BRU. Only make trial what your love can do   40
For Rome, towards Marcius.

MEN.   Well, and say that Marcius
Return me, as Cominius is return'd,
Unheard — what then?
But as a discontented friend, grief-shot
With his unkindness? Say't be so?

SIC.   Yet your good will 45
Must have that thanks from Rome after the measure
As you intended well.

MEN.   I'll undertake't.
I think he'll hear me. Yet, to bite his lip
And hum at good Cominius much unhearts me.
He was not taken well; he had not din'd. 50
The veins unfill'd, our blood is cold, and then
We pout upon the morning, are unapt
To give or to forgive; but when we have stuff'd
These pipes and these conveyances of our blood
With wine and feeding, we have suppler souls 55
Than in our priest-like fasts. Therefore I'll watch him
Till he be dieted to my request,
And then I'll set upon him.

BRU. You know the very road into his kindness
And cannot lose your way.

MEN.   Good faith, I'll prove him, 60
Speed how it will. I shall ere long have knowledge
Of my success.   *Exit.*

---

40 *make trial* test. 42 *Return me* send me away. 44 *grief-shot* stricken with grief. 46–7 *after . . . well* in proportion to your good intentions. 49 *hum at* greet with a "hum" — an expression of boredom and disdain. *unhearts* disheartens. 50 *He* Coriolanus. *taken well* approached at the right time. 51 *unfill'd* with food and drink. 52 *pout* look sourly, frown. 54 *conveyances* channels. 56 *watch* wait for. 57 *dieted to my request* sufficiently fed for me to make my plea. 60 *prove* attempt. 61 *Speed how it will* whatever the result may be. 62 *my success* how I have fared. 63 *in gold* upon a golden throne.

COM.   He'll never hear him.

SIC.   Not?

COM.   I tell you he does sit in gold, his eye
       Red as 'twould burn Rome, and his injury
       The jailer to his pity. I kneel'd before him.   65
       'Twas very faintly he said "Rise"; dismiss'd me
       Thus with his speechless hand. What he would do
       He sent in writing after me, what he would not,
       Bound with an oath to yield to his conditions;
       So that all hope is vain   70
       Unless in his noble mother and his wife,
       Who, as I hear, mean to solicit him
       For mercy to his country. Therefore let's hence
       And with our fair entreaties haste them on.   *Exeunt.*

◇◇◇◇◇◇◇◇◇◇◇◇◇◇◇

[SCENE II. *The Volscian camp before Rome.*]

Enter Menenius *to the* Watch *on guard.*

1. WATCH. Stay. Whence are you?

2. WATCH.   Stand, and go back.

MEN.   You guard like men; 'tis well. But, by your leave,
       I am an officer of state and come
       To speak with Coriolanus.

1. WATCH.   From whence?

MEN.   From Rome.

Plutarch reports that Coriolanus received the embassies from Rome seated in a great chair of state.   64 *Red* A red eye was a traditional sign of wrath. *injury* sense of injury.   65 *The . . . pity* keeping his feelings of pity from coming forth.   66 *faintly* languidly, with apparent unconcern.   68–9 *what he . . . conditions* This is a difficult textual crux, and it has been suggested that a line may be missing. The meaning seems to be "what he would not do (burn Rome) he swore to do if we did not yield to his terms."   71 *in his* it (hope) resides in his (κ; F¹: "his").
    V.II. 1 *Stay* stop.

1. WATCH. You may not pass; you must return. Our general   5
    Will no more hear from thence.

2. WATCH. You'll see your Rome embrac'd with fire before
    You'll speak with Coriolanus.

MEN.   Good my friends,
    If you have heard your general talk of Rome
    And of his friends there, it is lots to blanks   10
    My name hath touch'd your ears. It is Menenius.

1. WATCH. Be it so! Go back. The virtue of your name
    Is not here passable.

MEN.   I tell thee, fellow,
    Thy general is my lover. I have been
    The book of his good acts, whence men have read   15
    His fame unparallel'd, haply amplified;
    For I have ever verified my friends
    (Of whom he's chief) with all the size that verity
    Would without lapsing suffer. Nay, sometimes,
    Like to a bowl upon a subtle ground,   20
    I have tumbled past the throw, and in his praise
    Have (almost) stamp'd the leasing. Therefore, fellow,
    I must have leave to pass.

1. WATCH. Faith, sir, if you had told as many lies in his behalf as
    you have uttered words in your own, you should not pass   25
    here. No, though it were as virtuous to lie as to live
    chastely. Therefore go back.

MEN.   Prithee, fellow, remember my name is Menenius, always
    factionary on the party of your general.

2. WATCH. Howsoever you have been his liar, as you say you have,   30

---

10 *lots to blanks* a prize winning ticket in a lottery as opposed to a worthless one — i.e. a thousand to one shot.   12 *virtue* power.   13 *passable* (a)
valid currency (b) sufficient to allow you to pass.   14 *lover* friend.   15 *book*
record.   16 *haply* perhaps.   17 *verified* testified to the worth of.   18 *verity*
truth.   19 *lapsing* slipping, erring.   *suffer* permit.   20 *bowl* bowling ball.
subtle tricky.   21 *tumbled . . . throw* overshot the aimed-at distance.   22
stamp'd the leasing given the seal of truth to a lie.   26 *lie* (a) tell a falsehood
(b) lie down — with a bawdy quibble supported by "chastely."   29 *factionary on*

I am one that, telling true under him, must say you
cannot pass. Therefore go back.

MEN.   Has he din'd, canst thou tell? For I would not speak
with him till after dinner.

1. WATCH. You are a Roman, are you?   35

MEN.   I am, as thy general is.

1. WATCH. Then you should hate Rome, as he does. Can you,
when you have push'd out your gates the very defender
of them, and in a violent popular ignorance given your
enemy your shield, think to front his revenges with the   40
easy groans of old women, the virginal palms of your
daughters, or with the palsied intercession of such a
decay'd dotant as you seem to be? Can you think to
blow out the intended fire your city is ready to flame in
with such weak breath as this? No, you are deceiv'd.   45
Therefore, back to Rome and prepare for your execution. You are condemn'd; our general has sworn you out
of reprieve and pardon.

MEN.   Sirrah, if thy captain knew I were here, he would use
me with estimation.   50

1. WATCH. Come, my captain knows you not.

MEN.   I mean thy general.

1. WATCH. My general cares not for you. Back, I say, go! lest I let
forth your half-pint of blood. Back! That's the utmost
of your having. Back!   55

MEN.   Nay, but, fellow, fellow —

Enter Coriolanus *with* Aufidius.

---

an adherent to.   30 *Howsoever* even if you have.   *his liar* one who told lies for
him or about him.   31 *telling . . . him* telling the truth in his service.   39
in a . . . ignorance through the stupidity of mob violence.   40 *front* confront.
41 *easy groans* lamentations which require no effort.   *virginal palms* uplifted
hands of virgins.   43 *dotant* dotard, old man.   47-8 *sworn you out of* vowed that
you shall not have.   50 *estimation* proper respect.   53-4 *let forth* spill.   54-5
utmost of your having the most that you can take back with you.

COR.   What's the matter?

MEN.   Now, you companion, I'll say an errand for you. You
        shall know now that I am in estimation. You shall per-
        ceive that a Jack guardant cannot office me from my son
        Coriolanus. Guess, but by my entertainment with him,   60
        if thou stand'st not i' th' state of hanging, or of some
        death more long in spectatorship and crueller in suffer-
        ing. Behold now presently, and swoond for what's to
        come upon thee. [*To* Coriolanus] The glorious gods sit   65
        in hourly synod about thy particular prosperity and love
        thee no worse than thy old father Menenius does! O my
        son, my son! Thou art preparing fire for us. Look thee,
        here's water to quench it. I was hardly moved to come
        to thee; but being assured none but myself could move   70
        thee, I have been blown out of your gates with sighs,
        and conjure thee to pardon Rome and thy petitionary
        countrymen. The good gods assuage thy wrath, and turn
        the dregs of it upon this varlet here — this, who, like a
        block, hath denied my access to thee.   75

COR.   Away!

MEN.   How? Away?

COR.   Wife, mother, child I know not. My affairs
        Are servanted to others. Though I owe
        My revenge properly, my remission lies   80
        In Volscian breasts. That we have been familiar,
        Ingrate forgetfulness shall poison rather
        Than pity note how much. Therefore be gone.

---

58 *companion* rascal. *say an errand* deliver a message.   59 *in estimation* worthy
of respect.   60 *Jack guardant* knave (jack) on guard duty. *office me* keep me by
virtue of his office. A "Jack-in-office" was a common term for an officious person.
61 *but by my* MALONE; F¹: "but my." *entertainment with* reception by.   62 *i' th'
state* in the prospect, in danger.   63 *more . . . spectatorship* which takes longer
to watch — a more lingering death.   64 *presently* immediately. *swoond* faint
(in anticipation).   66 *synod* council. *particular* individual, personal.   69 *water*
tears. *hardly moved* persuaded with difficulty.   71 *your gates* those of your
native city (F¹; F⁴, K: "our gates"). The F⁴ reading obscures the poignancy of
Menenius's plea.   72 *petitionary* petitioning.   74 *dregs* poor remainder.   75

Mine ears against your suits are stronger than
Your gates against my force. Yet, for I lov'd thee,   85
Take this along. I writ it for thy sake   [*Gives a letter.*]
And would have sent it. Another word, Menenius,
I will not hear thee speak. This man, Aufidius,
Was my belov'd in Rome; yet thou behold'st.

AUF.   You keep a constant temper.   90

                    Exeunt. Manent the Guard *and* Me-
                    nenius.

1. WATCH. Now, sir, is your name Menenius?

2. WATCH. 'Tis a spell, you see, of much power. You know the way
          home again.

1. WATCH. Do you hear how we are shent for keeping your great-
          ness back?   95

2. WATCH. What cause do you think I have to swoond?

MEN.   I neither care for th' world nor your general; for such
         things as you, I can scarce think there's any, y'are so
         slight. He that hath a will to die by himself fears it not
         from another. Let your general do his worst. For you, be 100
         that you are, long; and your misery increase with your
         age! I say to you, as I was said to, "Away!"   *Exit.*

1. WATCH. A noble fellow, I warrant him.

2. WATCH. The worthy fellow is our general. He's the rock, the
          oak not to be wind-shaken.   *Exit* Watch. 105

---

block (a) blockhead (b) obstacle.   79 *servanted to* under the control of.   *owe*
possess.   80 *properly* myself.   *my remission* my power to forgive.   81 *familiar*
close to one another.   82–3 *Ingrate . . . how much* The ungrateful forgetfulness
of Coriolanus will poison the memory of their friendship, rather than his pity
cause him to acknowledge how close that friendship has been. This appears to be
the meaning, although some have held that the "forgetfulness" is that of
Menenius and the other Romans.   84 *stronger* more strongly barred.   85 *for*
because.   89 *belov'd* closest friend.   90 *constant temper* firm mind.   94 *shent*
scolded.   99 *slight* insignificant.   101 *that* what.

◇◇◇◇◇◇◇◇◇◇◇◇◇◇◇

[SCENE III. *The Tent of* Coriolanus.]

Enter Coriolanus *and* Aufidius, [*with others*].

COR.   We will before the walls of Rome to-morrow
Set down our host. My partner in this action,
You must report to th' Volscian lords how plainly
I have borne this business.

AUF.   Only their ends
You have respected; stopp'd your ears against   5
The general suit of Rome; never admitted
A private whisper — no, not with such friends
That thought them sure of you.

COR.   This last old man,
Whom with a crack'd heart I have sent to Rome,
Lov'd me above the measure of a father;   10
Nay, godded me indeed. Their latest refuge
Was to send him; for whose old love I have
(Though I show'd sourly to him) once more offer'd
The first conditions, which they did refuse
And cannot now accept. To grace him only   15
That thought he could do more, a very little
I have yielded to. Fresh embassies and suits,
Nor from the state nor private friends, hereafter
Will I lend ear to. (*Shout within.*) Ha! what shout is this?
Shall I be tempted to infringe my vow   20
In the same time 'tis made? I will not.

V.III. 2 *Set down* encamp. *host* army.   3 *plainly* openly, in a straightforward
manner.   4 *borne* conducted. *their ends* those of the Volscians.   6 *suit* petition.
11 *godded* deified. *latest refuge* final resort.   13 *show'd* looked.   15 *grace*
gratify.   17–18 *Fresh embassies . . . friends* neither fresh embassies from the
government nor pleas from my personal friends.   22–3 *mould . . . fram'd* my
mother.   24 *affection* natural feeling.   25 *All bond . . . break* let every bond
that ties me to wife, mother and child and every claim that natural feeling makes

Enter Virgilia, Volumnia, Valeria,
Young Marcius, *with* Attendants.

My wife comes foremost; then the honour'd mould
Wherein this trunk was fram'd, and in her hand
The grandchild to her blood. But out, affection!
All bond and privilege of nature, break!   25
Let it be virtuous to be obstinate.
What is that curtsy worth? or those dove's eyes,
Which can make gods forsworn? I melt and am not
Of stronger earth than others. My mother bows,
As if Olympus to a molehill should   30
In supplication nod; and my young boy
Hath an aspect of intercession which
Great Nature cries "Deny not." — Let the Volsces
Plough Rome and harrow Italy! I'll never
Be such a gosling to obey instinct, but stand   35
As if a man were author of himself
And knew no other kin.

VIR.   My lord and husband!

COR.   These eyes are not the same I wore in Rome.

VIR.   The sorrow that delivers us thus chang'd
Makes you think so.

COR.   Like a dull actor now,   40
I have forgot my part and I am out,
Even to a full disgrace. Best of my flesh,
Forgive my tyranny; but do not say
For that, "Forgive our Romans." O, a kiss
Long as my exile, sweet as my revenge!   45
Now by the jealous queen of heaven, that kiss
I carried from thee, dear, and my true lip
Hath virgin'd it e'er since. You gods! I prate

---

upon me be severed.   28 *forsworn* breakers of oaths.   32 *aspect of intercession*
pleading look.   35 *stand* persist, remain constant.   36 *author* creator.   38
These eyes . . . in Rome I see the world differently from when I was in Rome.
39 *delivers* reveals.   41 *out* at fault.   43 *tyranny* cruelty.   46 *queen of heaven*
Juno, the patron goddess of marriage and proverbially jealous.   48 *prate* speak
foolishly (THEOBALD; F¹: "pray").

And the most noble mother of the world
Leave unsaluted. Sink, my knee, i' th' earth;   *Kneels.* 50
Of thy deep duty more impression show
Than that of common sons.

VOL.   O, stand up bless'd!

                         [*Raises him.*]

Whilst with no softer cushion than the flint
I kneel before thee, and unproperly
Show duty, as mistaken all this while   55
Between the child and parent.   [*Kneels; he raises her.*]

COR.   What is this?
Your knees to me? to your corrected son?
Then let the pebbles on the hungry beach
Fillop the stars! Then let the mutinous winds
Strike the proud cedars 'gainst the fiery sun,   60
Murd'ring impossibility, to make
What cannot be, slight work!

VOL.   Thou art my warrior;
I holp to frame thee. Do you know this lady?

COR. The noble sister of Publicola,
The moon of Rome, chaste as the icicle   65
That curded by the frost from purest snow
And hangs on Dian's temple! Dear Valeria!

VOL. This is a poor epitome of yours,
Which by th' interpretation of full time
May show like all yourself.

COR.   The god of soldiers,   70
With the consent of supreme Jove, inform

---

57 *corrected* chastened (by Volumnia's speech).   59 *Fillop* strike against.   61
Murd'ring impossibility making anything possible. If a mother can kneel to a
son, then no calamity of nature is beyond possibility.   62 *slight work* an easy
task.   63 *holp* helped.   65 *moon* proverbial symbol of chastity.   66 *curded*
congealed (K; F¹: "curdied").   67 *Dian* Diana, goddess of virginity.   68 *This*
young Marcius.   *epitome* small model (literally, a small edition).   69 *by . . .
time* when time shall have interpreted him fully (revealed what he is to be). The
image of the "epitome" as a text to be interpreted is carried out.   70 *god of
soldiers* Mars.   71 *inform* inspire.   73 *stick* stand out prominently.   74 *seamark*

Thy thoughts with nobleness, that thou mayst prove
To shame unvulnerable, and stick i' th' wars
Like a great seamark, standing every flaw
And saving those that eye thee!

VOL.   Your knee, sirrah.   75

COR.   That's my brave boy!

VOL.   Even he, your wife, this lady, and myself
Are suitors to you.

COR.   I beseech you, peace!
Or, if you'ld ask, remember this before:
The thing I have forsworn to grant may never   80
Be held by you denials. Do not bid me
Dismiss my soldiers or capitulate
Again with Rome's mechanics. Tell me not
Wherein I seem unnatural. Desire not
T' allay my rages and revenges with   85
Your colder reasons.

VOL.   O, no more, no more!
You have said you will not grant us anything;
For we have nothing else to ask but that
Which you deny already: yet we will ask,
That, if you fail in our request, the blame   90
May hang upon your hardness. Therefore hear us.

COR.   Aufidius, and you Volsces, mark; for we'll
Hear naught from Rome in private. — Your request?

VOL.   Should we be silent and not speak, our raiment
And state of bodies would bewray what life   95
We have led since thy exile. Think with thyself
How more unfortunate than all living women

---

landmark used by navigators to check their positions at sea. *standing* with-
standing. *flaw* strong gust of wind.   75 *eye thee* look to thee for guidance (as
the seamark is looked to by the navigator).   76 *brave* fine.   80 *forsworn to* sworn
not to.   81 *Be . . . denials* be considered by you as a refusal to grant your
requests.   82 *capitulate* negotiate, draw up terms of agreement.   84-5 *Desire
. . . allay* do not ask me to assuage.   86 *colder* calmer, less impassioned.   90
fail fail us. 94-5 *raiment . . . bodies* ragged clothes and emaciated bodies.   95
bewray reveal.

Are we come hither; since that thy sight, which should
Make our eyes flow with joy, hearts dance with comforts,
Constrains them weep and shake with fear and sorrow,   100
Making the mother, wife, and child to see
The son, the husband, and the father tearing
His country's bowels out. And to poor we
Thine enmity 's most capital. Thou barr'st us
Our prayers to the gods, which is a comfort   105
That all but we enjoy. For how can we,
Alas, how can we for our country pray,
Whereto we are bound, together with thy victory,
Whereto we are bound? Alack, or we must lose
The country, our dear nurse, or else thy person,   110
Our comfort in the country. We must find
An evident calamity, though we had
Our wish, which side should win; for either thou
Must as a foreign recreant be led
With manacles thorough our streets, or else   115
Triumphantly tread on thy country's ruin
And bear the palm for having bravely shed
Thy wife and children's blood. For myself, son,
I purpose not to wait on fortune till
These wars determine. If I cannot persuade thee   120
Rather to show a noble grace to both parts
Than seek the end of one, thou shalt no sooner
March to assault thy country than to tread
(Trust to't, thou shalt not) on thy mother's womb
That brought thee to this world.

VIR.   Ay, and on mine,   125
That brought you forth this boy to keep your name
Living to time.

BOY.   'A shall not tread on me!

---

100 *Constrains them* forces them to.   103 *poor we* poor us. The grammar is
unusual but not without precedent.   104 *capital* fatal. *barr'st us* keepest us
from.   111 *find* endure.   112 *evident* manifest.   114 *recreant* traitor.   117 *palm*
emblem of victory.   120 *determine* are concluded.   121 *parts* sides — Roman
and Volscian.   129–30 *Not of . . . to see* for a man to avoid becoming as tender
as a woman, he must refrain from looking upon a child's or woman's face.   135

I'll run away till I am bigger, but then I'll fight.

COR.   Not of a woman's tenderness to be
Requires nor child nor woman's face to see.   130
I have sat too long.   [*Rises.*]

VOL.   Nay, go not from us thus!
If it were so that our request did tend
To save the Romans, thereby to destroy
The Volsces whom you serve, you might condemn us
As poisonous of your honour. No! our suit   135
Is that you reconcile them while the Volsces
May say "This mercy we have show'd," the Romans,
"This we receiv'd," and each in either side
Give the all-hail to thee and cry "Be blest
For making up this peace!" Thou know'st, great son,   140
The end of war 's uncertain, but this certain,
That, if thou conquer Rome, the benefit
Which thou shalt thereby reap is such a name
Whose repetition will be dogg'd with curses,
Whose chronicle thus writ, "The man was noble,   145
But with his last attempt he wip'd it out,
Destroy'd his country, and his name remains
To th' ensuing age abhorr'd." Speak to me, son.
Thou hast affected the fine strains of honour,
To imitate the graces of the gods,   150
To tear with thunder the wide cheeks o' th' air,
And yet to charge thy sulphur with a bolt
That should but rive an oak. Why dost not speak?
Think'st thou it honourable for a noble man
Still to remember wrongs? Daughter, speak you.   155
He cares not for your weeping. Speak thou, boy.
Perhaps thy childishness will move him more

---

poisonous of destructive to.   139 *all-hail* shout of acclamation.   149 *affected*
loved.   *fine* JOHNSON; F¹: "fiue."   152 *charge* load (WARBURTON; F¹: "change").
sulphur lightning.   153 *rive* split.   *an oak* The point is that the gods, while
they thunder loudly, direct their thunderbolts only against the stoutest trees, such
as the oaks; they threaten, but they are merciful to the weak.   155 *Still* forever.

Than can our reasons. There's no man in the world
More bound to 's mother; yet here he lets me prate
Like one i' th' stocks. Thou hast never in thy life   160
Show'd thy dear mother any courtesy,
When she (poor hen), fond of no second brood,
Has cluck'd thee to the wars, and safely home
Loaden with honour. Say my request 's unjust,
And spurn me back. But if it be not so,   165
Thou art not honest, and the gods will plague thee
That thou restrain'st from me the duty which
To a mother's part belongs. He turns away.
Down, ladies! Let us shame him with our knees.
To his surname Coriolanus 'longs more pride   170
Than pity to our prayers. Down! An end!

                                        [*They kneel.*]

This is the last. So, we will home to Rome
And die among our neighbours. Nay, behold 's!
This boy, that cannot tell what he would have
But kneels and holds up hands for fellowship,   175
Does reason our petition with more strength
Than thou hast to deny't. Come, let us go.   [*They rise.*]
This fellow had a Volscian to his mother;
His wife is in Corioles, and this child
Like him by chance. Yet give us our dispatch.   180
I am hush'd until our city be afire.
And then I'll speak a little.

                [He] holds her by the hand, silent.

COR.   O mother, mother!
What have you done? Behold, the heavens do ope,

---

159 *prate* talk idly.   160 *Like . . . stocks* like one being publicly humiliated. No
one heeded the talk of such vagabonds as were usually imprisoned in the stocks.
162 *fond of* desiring.   164 *Loaden* laden.   166 *honest* honourable, true to yourself.   167–8 *That thou . . . belongs* because you withhold from me the duteous
respect (of her son) which is a mother's natural right.   169 *him with* F²; F¹: "him
with him with."   170 *'longs* belongs.   173 *behold's* look at us. Coriolanus apparently has turned away his eyes.   174 *cannot tell* does not really understand.
175 *for fellowship* for the sake of partnership (with us).   176 *reason* argue.   180
dispatch dismissal.   182 S.D. *[He] holds . . . silent* This is one of the most ex-
pressive stage directions in all of Shakespeare. Shakespeare is following Plutarch

The gods look down, and this unnatural scene
They laugh at. O my mother, mother! O!   185
You have won a happy victory to Rome;
But for your son — believe it, O believe it! —
Most dangerously you have with him prevail'd,
If not most mortal to him. But let it come.
Aufidius, though I cannot make true wars,   190
I'll frame convenient peace. Now, good Aufidius,
Were you in my stead, would you have heard
A mother less? or granted less, Aufidius?

AUF.   I was mov'd withal.

COR.   I dare be sworn you were!
And, sir, it is no little thing to make   195
Mine eyes to sweat compassion. But, good sir,
What peace you'll make, advise me. For my part,
I'll not to Rome, I'll back with you; and pray you
Stand to me in this cause. O mother! wife!

AUF.   [aside] I am glad thou hast set thy mercy and thy honour 200
At difference in thee. Out of that I'll work
Myself a former fortune.

COR.   Ay, by-and-by.
But we will drink together; and you shall bear
A better witness back than words, which we,
On like conditions, will have counterseal'd.   205
Come, enter with us. Ladies, you deserve
To have a temple built you. All the swords
In Italy, and her confederate arms,
Could not have made this peace.   *Exeunt.*

closely.   189 *mortal* fatally. Coriolanus sees that his own death must result from
his giving in to his mother's plea.   191 *convenient* suitable.   192 *stead* place
(F⁴; F¹: "steed").   196 *sweat compassion* weep tears of pity. Tears and perspiration
were believed to consist of the same substance.   199 *Stand to* support.   201 *At
difference* in conflict.   201-2 *I'll work . . . fortune* I will restore my position to
what it was formerly (before I shared the generalship with Coriolanus).   204
better . . . words i.e. a written rather than an oral agreement.   204-5 *which we
. . . counterseal'd* a treaty which we, having agreed on the same conditions, will
both have sealed.   208 *confederate arms* allied military forces.

◇◇◇◇◇◇◇◇◇◇◇◇◇◇◇◇

[SCENE IV. *Rome. A public place.*]

Enter Menenius *and* Sicinius.

MEN. See you yond coign o' th' Capitol, yond cornerstone?

SIC. Why, what of that?

MEN. If it be possible for you to displace it with your little
finger, there is some hope the ladies of Rome, especially
his mother, may prevail with him. But I say there is no   5
hope in't. Our throats are sentenc'd and stay upon execution.

SIC. Is't possible that so short a time can alter the condition
of a man?

MEN. There is difference between a grub and a butterfly; yet   10
your butterfly was a grub. This Marcius is grown from
man to dragon. He has wings; he's more than a creeping
thing.

SIC. He lov'd his mother dearly.

MEN. So did he me; and he no more remembers his mother now   15
than an eight-year-old horse. The tartness of his face
sours ripe grapes. When he walks, he moves like an engine, and the ground shrinks before his treading. He is
able to pierce a corslet with his eye, talks like a knell,
and his hum is a battery. He sits in his state, as a thing   20
made for Alexander. What he bids be done is finish'd
with his bidding. He wants nothing of a god but eternity
and a heaven to throne in.

V.IV. 1 *coign* corner.   6 *stay upon* await.   8 *condition* character.   10 *dif-
ferency* a difference.   17–18 *engine* battering-ram, a heavy, lumbering instrument
of war.   19 *corslet* breastplate.   *knell* death knell.   20 *hum* mere grunt.   *is a
battery* constitutes an assault.   *state* chair of state, throne.   20–1 *as . . .
Alexander* as though he were a statue of Alexander the Great.   22 *with his
bidding* as soon as it has been ordered.   *wants nothing* lacks no attribute.   25

SIC.   Yes, mercy, if you report him truly.

MEN.   I paint him in the character. Mark what mercy his   25
mother shall bring from him. There is no more mercy in
him than there is milk in a male tiger. That shall our
poor city find; and all this is long of you.

SIC.   The gods be good unto us!

MEN.   No, in such a case the gods will not be good unto us.   30
When we banish'd him, we respected not them; and, he
returning to break our necks, they respect not us.

Enter a Messenger.

MESS.   Sir, if you'ld save your life, fly to your house.
The plebeians have got your fellow tribune
And hale him up and down; all swearing, if   35
The Roman ladies bring not comfort home,
They'll give him death by inches.

Enter another Messenger.

SIC.   What's the news?

MESS.   Good news, good news! The ladies have prevail'd,
The Volscians are dislodg'd, and Marcius gone.
A merrier day did never yet greet Rome;   40
No, not th' expulsion of the Tarquins.

SIC.   Friend,
Art thou certain this is true? Is it most certain?

MESS.   As certain as I know the sun is fire.
Where have you lurk'd that you make doubt of it?
Ne'er through an arch so hurried the blown tide   45
As the recomforted through th' gates. Why, hark you!

*Trumpets, hautboys; drums beat; all
together.*

---

in the character accurately, according to what he really is.   28 *long of* because of.
35 *hale him* drag him violently.   37 *death by inches* a slow, lingering means of
death.   39 *dislodg'd* departed from their camp, lifted their seige.   44 *lurk'd*
been hiding.   45 *arch* of a bridge. Shakespeare may be thinking of the waters
flowing between the arches of London Bridge. *blown* swollen.   46 s.d. *hautboys*
oboes.

The trumpets, sackbuts, psalteries, and fifes,
Tabors and cymbals and the shouting Romans
Make the sun dance. Hark you!   *A shout within.*

MEN.   This is good news.
I will go meet the ladies. This Volumnia   50
Is worth of consuls, senators, patricians,
A city full; of tribunes such as you,
A sea and land full. You have pray'd well to-day.
This morning for ten thousand of your throats
I'd not have given a doit. Hark, how they joy!   55

Sound still with the shouts.

SIC.   First, the gods bless you for your tidings; next,
Accept my thankfulness.

MESS.   Sir, we have all
Great cause to give great thanks.

SIC.   They are near the city.

MESS.   Almost at point to enter.

SIC.   We will meet them
And help the joy.   *Exeunt.* 60

◇◇◇◇◇◇◇◇◇◇◇◇◇◇◇◇◇◇

[SCENE V. *Rome. A street near the gate.*]

Enter two Senators, *with* Ladies, [Volumnia, Virgilia,
Valeria,] *passing over the stage, with other* Lords.

SENATOR. Behold our patroness, the life of Rome!
Call all your tribes together, praise the gods,
And make triumphant fires; strew flowers before them.

---

47 *sackbuts* musical instruments related to the trombone. *psalteries* stringed instruments.   48 *Tabors* small drums.   49 *sun dance* the ultimate sign of joy and celebration, since according to popular superstition the sun danced on Easter morning.   55 *doit* a half farthing coin.   59 *at point* about.   60 *help the joy* add to the merriment.

V.v. 2 *tribes* divisions of the Roman populace.   3 *triumphant fires* Bonfires

Unshout the noise that banish'd Marcius;
Repeal him with the welcome of his mother.   5
Cry, "Welcome, ladies, welcome!"

ALL.   Welcome, ladies,
    Welcome!

A flourish with drums and trumpets.
[Exeunt.]

❖❖❖❖❖❖❖❖❖❖❖❖❖

[SCENE VI. *Corioles. A public place.*]

Enter Tullus Aufidius, *with* Attendants.

AUF.   Go tell the lords o' th' city I am here.
    Deliver them this paper. Having read it,
    Bid them repair to th' market place, where I,
    Even in theirs and in the commons' ears,
    Will vouch the truth of it. Him I accuse   5
    The city ports by this hath enter'd and
    Intends t' appear before the people, hoping
    To purge himself with words. Dispatch.

                        [*Exeunt* Attendants.]

            Enter three or four Conspirators *of*
            Aufidius' *faction.*

                        Most welcome!

1. CON.   How is it with our general?

AUF.   Even so
    As with a man by his own alms empoison'd   10
    And with his charity slain.

were traditional symbols of victory.   4 *Unshout* cancel by means of even greater
shouting (ROWE; F¹: "Vnshoot").   5 *Repeal him* call him back from exile.
   V.VI. 5 *Him I accuse* he whom I accuse.   6 *ports* gates. *by this* by this time.
8 *purge* exonerate. *with words* with mere words (as opposed to his previous
actions). *Dispatch* make haste.

2. CON.   Most noble sir,
If you do hold the same intent wherein
You wish'd us parties, we'll deliver you
Of your great danger.

AUF.   Sir, I cannot tell.
We must proceed as we do find the people.   15

3. CON.   The people will remain uncertain whilst
'Twixt you there's difference; but the fall of either
Makes the survivor heir of all.

AUF.   I know it;
And my pretext to strike at him admits
A good construction. I rais'd him, and I pawn'd   20
Mine honour for his truth; who being so heighten'd,
He watered his new plants with dews of flattery,
Seducing so my friends; and to this end
He bow'd his nature, never known before
But to be rough, unswayable, and free.   25

3. CON.   Sir, his stoutness
When he did stand for consul, which he lost
By lack of stooping —

AUF.   That I would have spoke of.
Being banish'd for't, he came unto my hearth,
Presented to my knife his throat. I took him;   30
Made him joint-servant with me; gave him way
In all his own desires; nay, let him choose
Out of my files, his projects to accomplish,
My best and freshest men; serv'd his designments
In mine own person; holp to reap the fame   35

---

13 *parties* to be confederates.   *deliver* free. The metaphor is drawn from child-birth.   15 *as we . . . people* according to what we find the people's disposition to be.   19–20 *admits . . . construction* allows for favourable interpretation.   20 *rais'd him* gave him high office.   *pawn'd* pledged.   21 *truth* loyalty.   *heighten'd* exalted.   22–3 *He watered . . . friends* That Coriolanus should have gained favour with the Volscians by flattery seems inconsistent with what we have been shown of his behaviour in Rome, and Aufidius is thus held by most commentators to be lying. But Shakespeare does not make this clear. Perhaps he is suggesting that Coriolanus, once he had embraced his enemies, lost that very virtue which made him incapable of stooping to flattery while in Rome. The

Which he did end all his, and took some pride
To do myself this wrong; till at the last
I seem'd his follower, not partner, and
He wag'd me with his countenance as if
I had been mercenary.

1. CON.   So he did, my lord.   40
The army marvell'd at it; and, in the last,
When he had carried Rome and that we look'd
For no less spoil than glory —

AUF.   There was it!
For which my sinews shall be stretch'd upon him.
At a few drops of women's rheum, which are   45
As cheap as lies, he sold the blood and labour
Of our great action. Therefore shall he die,
And I'll renew me in his fall. But hark!

*Drums and trumpets sound, with great
shouts of the people.*

1. CON. Your native town you enter'd like a post
And had no welcomes home; but he returns   50
Splitting the air with noise.

2. CON.   And patient fools,
Whose children he hath slain, their base throats tear
With giving him glory.

3. CON.   Therefore, at your vantage,
Ere he express himself or move the people
With what he would say, let him feel your sword,   55

---

matter is far from clear.   24 *bow'd his nature* lowered his natural character.
25 *unswayable* incapable of being ruled. *free* outspoken and honest.   26 *stoutness* stubbornness.   31 *joint-servant* partner. *way* his way.   33 *files* ranks of
men.   34 *designments* designs, enterprises.   35 *holp* helped.   36 *end all his*
harvest all for his own (carrying on the metaphor of "reap").   39–40 *He wag'd
. . . mercenary* he repaid (wag'd) me with his patronizing looks as though I
were merely his hired man.   41 *in the last* finally.   42 *carried* virtually defeated.   44 *my sinews . . . him* my every nerve will be strained to defeat him.
45 *rheum* tears.   46 *blood and labour* bloody labour.   48 *renew me* be reborn,
attain my former grandeur.   49 *post* messenger.   53 *vantage* opportunity.

Which we will second. When he lies along,
After your way his tale pronounc'd shall bury
His reasons with his body.

AUF.　　　　　　　　　　　　　　Say no more.
Here come the lords.

Enter the Lords *of the city.*

ALL LORDS. You are most welcome home.

AUF.　　　　　　　　　　　　　I have not deserv'd it.　60
But, worthy lords, have you with heed perus'd
What I have written to you?

ALL.　　　　　　　　　　　　　We have.

1. LORD.　　　　　　　　　　　And grieve to hear't.
What faults he made before the last, I think
Might have found easy fines; but there to end
Where he was to begin, and give away　　　　65
The benefit of our levies, answering us
With our own charge, making a treaty where
There was a yielding — this admits no excuse.

AUF.　He approaches. You shall hear him.

Enter Coriolanus, *marching with*
Drum *and* Colours, *the* Commoners
being with him.

COR.　Hail, lords! I am return'd your soldier;　　70
No more infected with my country's love
Than when I parted hence, but still subsisting
Under your great command. You are to know

---

56 *second* support (with our swords). *lies along* lies low, has fallen.　57 *After*
. . . *pronounc'd* his story according to your own version of it.　58 *reasons* justifi-
cations (of his actions).　61 *with heed* carefully.　64 *easy fines* light penalties.
64–5 *end . . . begin* i.e. stop fighting where he should have begun, with the sack
of Rome.　65–6 *give . . . levies* give up the spoils (benefit) which should have
been our return for all our expenses (levies) in raising an army.　66–7 *answering*
. . . *charge* repaying us by merely returning to us the power and office we had
given him.　67–8 *making . . . yielding* coming to terms when the enemy had

That prosperously I have attempted, and
With bloody passage led your wars even to   75
The gates of Rome. Our spoils we have brought home
Doth more than counterpoise a full third part
The charges of the action. We have made peace
With no less honour to the Antiates
Than shame to th' Romans; and we here deliver,   80
Subscrib'd by th' consuls and patricians,
Together with the seal o' th' Senate, what
We have compounded on.

AUF.   Read it not, noble lords;
But tell the traitor in the highest degree
He hath abus'd your powers.   85

COR.   Traitor? How now?

AUF.   Ay, traitor, Marcius.

COR.   Marcius?

AUF.   Ay, Marcius, Caius Marcius! Dost thou think
I'll grace thee with that robbery, thy stol'n name
Coriolanus, in Corioles?
You lords and heads o' th' state, perfidiously   90
He has betray'd your business and given up,
For certain drops of salt, your city Rome
(I say "your city") to his wife and mother;
Breaking his oath and resolution like
A twist of rotten silk; never admitting   95
Counsel o' th' war; but at his nurse's tears
He whin'd and roar'd away your victory,
That pages blush'd at him, and men of heart

_____

already surrendered.   68 *admits* allows of.   71 *infected* influenced by.   72
subsisting continuing.   74 *prosperously I have attempted* my military enterprise
has been successful.   77 *counterpoise* equal in weight.   78 *charges* expenses.
action campaign.   79 *Antiates* citizens of Antium.   83 *compounded* agreed.   84
traitor . . . degree worst kind of traitor.   92 *drops of salt* tears (of Volumnia
and the other pleaders).   95 *twist* strand.   95-6 *admitting . . . war* consulting
his fellow military commanders.   98 *That* so that.   *men of heart* brave men.

Look'd wond'ring each at other.

COR.   Hear'st thou, Mars?

AUF.   Name not the god, thou boy of tears!

COR.   Ha!   100

AUF.   No more.

COR.   Measureless liar, thou hast made my heart
Too great for what contains it. Boy? O slave!
Pardon me, lords; 'tis the first time that ever
I was forc'd to scold. Your judgments, my grave lords,   105
Must give this cur the lie; and his own notion —
Who wears my stripes impress'd upon him, that
Must bear my beating to his grave — shall join
To thrust the lie unto him.

1. LORD. Peace both, and hear me speak.   110

COR.   Cut me to pieces, Volsces. Men and lads,
Stain all your edges on me. Boy? False hound!
If you have writ your annals true, 'tis there,
That, like an eagle in a dovecote, I
Flutter'd your Volscians in Corioles.   115
Alone I did it. Boy?

AUF.   Why, noble lords,
Will you be put in mind of his blind fortune,
Which was your shame, by this unholy braggart?
Fore your own eyes and ears?

ALL CONSPIRATORS.   Let him die for't!

ALL PEOPLE. Tear him to pieces! — Do it presently! — He kill'd my 120
son! — My daughter! — He kill'd my cousin Marcus! —
He kill'd my father!

---

99 *each at other* at each other. *Mars* the god of war, whom Coriolanus would
think of as his particular patron deity.   100 *boy of tears* weeping child, crybaby.
To call a man a "boy" is a great insult; this compounds the insult.   101 *No
more* merely a crybaby.   103 *what contains it* my body.   106 *notion* reason,
common sense.   107 *stripes* signs of whipping. Coriolanus is being contemptuous
in using a term associated with this kind of punishment.   112 *Stain* with blood.
edges swords.   113 *your annals* the history of your city. *true* accurately.   115
Flutter'd F³; F¹: "Flatter'd."   116 *Alone* Thus Shakespeare at the end emphasizes

2. LORD. Peace, ho! No outrage! Peace!
    The man is noble, and his fame folds in
    This orb o' th' earth. His last offences to us   125
    Shall have judicious hearing. Stand, Aufidius,
    And trouble not the peace.

COR.   O that I had him,
    With six Aufidiuses, or more — his tribe,
    To use my lawful sword!

AUF.   Insolent villain!

ALL CONSPIRATORS. Kill, kill, kill, kill, kill him!

          Draw the Conspirators, *and kill* Mar-
          cius, *who falls.* Aufidius *stands on him.*

LORDS.   Hold, hold, hold, hold!   130

AUF.   My noble masters, hear me speak.

1. LORD.   O Tullus!

2. LORD. Thou hast done a deed whereat valour will weep.

3. LORD. Tread not upon him. Masters all, be quiet!
    Put up your swords.

AUF.   My lords, when you shall know (as in this rage   135
    Provok'd by him you cannot) the great danger
    Which this man's life did owe you, you'll rejoice
    That he is thus cut off. Please it your Honours
    To call me to your Senate, I'll deliver
    Myself your loyal servant or endure   140
    Your heaviest censure.

1. LORD.   Bear from hence his body,
    And mourn you for him. Let him be regarded

---

the solitude which has been the mark of Coriolanus throughout his career.   117
put in mind reminded.   *blind fortune* mere luck.   119 *Fore* before.   120
presently at once.   124–5 *folds in . . . earth* encompasses the entire earth, is
universal.   126 *judicious hearing* a legal trial.   *Stand* stand aside.   128 *tribe*
entire family.   137 *Which . . . owe you* which while he lived this man held in
store for you — and thus would eventually have come to you.   139 *deliver*
demonstrate.   141 *heaviest censure* severest condemnation.

As the most noble corse that ever herald
Did follow to his urn.

2. LORD.   His own impatience
Takes from Aufidius a great part of blame.   145
Let's make the best of it.

AUF.   My rage is gone,
And I am struck with sorrow. Take him up.
Help three o' th' chiefest soldiers; I'll be one.
Beat thou the drum that it speak mournfully.
Trail your steel pikes. Though in this city he   150
Hath widowed and unchilded many a one,
Which to this hour bewail the injury,
Yet he shall have a noble memory.
Assist.

Exeunt, bearing the body of Marcius.
A dead march sounded.

143-4 *herald . . . urn* At Elizabethan funerals of important persons it was
customary for a herald to proclaim the rank and station of the dead person at
the conclusion of the funeral ceremony.   148 *one* one pallbearer. On the Elizabethan stage four men were usually used to carry off dead bodies.   150 *Trail . . .
pikes* A customary detail in military funerals.   151 *unchilded* deprived of
children.   153 *memory* memorial.